What people are say

Near Death Experiences and Sacred Scripture: The Parallel Messaging

Drawing skillfully on comparative religion and the well established material on Near Death Experiences, Professor Hodgson has created an extremely interesting and compelling account. I strongly suspect you will, like me, find that it contains numerous universal truths for contemplation. I honestly and thoroughly recommend this fascinating book which has the Golden Rule at its very core.

—**John Davey**, Retired Psychologist and President of the Theosophical Society in Western Australia

Professor Hodgson's thought-provoking book is a captivating exploration of the messaging parallels between near-death experiences and sacred teachings. Readers will discover new understandings and interpretations concerning the ultimate reality and the interconnectedness of all beings. Professor Hodgson's book also provides solace and strength to people faced with modern challenges by restoring their hope and reigniting their faith in God, the afterlife, existential mysteries and universal laws such as karma and reincarnation.

—**Dr Lance Storm**, Research Fellow, School of Psychology, University of Adelaide, South Australia, Committee Member, Australian Institute of Parasychological Research

Many people are unaware that the word religion means social bond. Why then do people over-focus on perceived intra-religious and inter-religious differences rather than the amazing number of similarities in world religions? I would like to recommend the book *Near Death Experiences and Sacred Scripture: The Parallel*

Messaging to people interested in thanatology (the study of death and the needs of the terminally ill and their families), clerics and the general public. I found it both inspiring and refreshing, so will you.

—**Dr Chris Johnson**, Clinical Professor of Sociology, Texas State University; editor of *How Different Religions View Death and Afterlife* (3rd edition, 2018, XanEdu Press)

Near Death Experiences and Sacred Scripture

The Parallel Messaging

Near Death Experiences and Sacred Scripture

The Parallel Messaging

By Douglas Charles Hodgson

BOOKS

London, UK
Washington, DC, USA

CollectiveInk

First published by O-Books, 2024
O-Books is an imprint of Collective Ink Ltd.,
Unit 11, Shepperton House, 89 Shepperton Road, London, N1 3DF
office@collectiveinkbooks.com
www.collectiveinkbooks.com
www.o-books.com

For distributor details and how to order please visit the 'Ordering' section on our website.

Text copyright: Douglas Charles Hodgson 2023

ISBN: 978 1 80341 575 8
978 1 80341 587 1 (ebook)
Library of Congress Control Number: 2023908598

A CIP catalogue record for this book is available from the British Library.

Design: Lapiz Digital Services

UK: Printed and bound by CPI Group (UK) Ltd, Croydon, CR0 4YY
Printed in North America by CPI GPS partners

Portions of Chapter 4 reference Cheri Huber's work, including her "recording and listening" practice, reprinted by permission of Living Compassion (Cheri Huber).
Portions of Chapter 8 reference Julian Treasure's Ted Talk "5 Ways to Listen Better," reprinted by permission of Julian Treasure, with his name and link to his website; and Sanni Honnold's "Effective Communication: How to Have a Hard Conversation" workshop, reprinted by permission of Sanni Honnold.

The author of this book does not dispense medical advice or
prescribe the use of any technique as a form of treatment for
physical, emotional, or medical problems without the advice of a
physician, either directly or indirectly. The intent of the author
is only to offer information of a general nature to help you in
your quest for emotional and spiritual well-being. In the event
you use any of the information in this book for yourself, which is
your constitutional right, the author and the publisher assume no
responsibility for your actions.

We operate a distinctive and ethical publishing philosophy in
all areas of our business, from our global network of authors to
production and worldwide distribution.

Table of Contents

Strive not to be perfect but rather to be better.
—Chandra Kala Rai

The human mystery is incredibly demeaned by scientific reductionism ... we have to recognize that we are spiritual beings with souls existing in a spiritual world as well as material beings with bodies and brains existing in a material world.
—Sir John Eccles

Consciousness precedes Being and not the other way around. For this reason, the salvation of this human world lies nowhere else than within the human heart.
—Václav Havel

A human being is part of the whole called by us universe, a part limited in time and space. We experience ourselves, our thoughts and feelings as something separate from the rest. A kind of optical delusion of consciousness. The delusion is a kind of prison for us, restricting us to our personal desires and to affection for a few persons nearest to us. Our task must be to free ourselves from the prison by widening our circle of compassion to embrace all living creatures and the whole of nature in its beauty. The true value of a human being is determined by the measure and sense in which they have obtained liberation from the self. We shall require a substantially new manner of thinking if humanity is to survive.
—Albert Einstein

Seek the Creator of all Creation who created you to find Him. Desire to know your Creator and all things will be added unto you.
—Anonymous Near Death Experiencer

Every living thing will find its own perfection with unconditional love.

—Words spoken by a Being of Light to an Anonymous Near Death Experiencer

The love you give is yours for eternity. All you can carry with you upon your death is the love you have given to others.

—Anonymous Near Death Experiencer

What the eye can see is of no lasting value; what the eye cannot see is priceless beyond comprehension.

—Douglas Charles Hodgson

Preface

Many of us consider only fleetingly, and seldom profoundly, certain of life's larger questions. Does God exist? What happens when I die? Is there an afterlife? Does Heaven exist and, if so, what is it like? What other spiritual realms and dimensions exist? Do I possess an eternal soul or consciousness that survives the death of my physical body? And how may I liberate my soul-consciousness from illusion and delusion? What is the purpose of my Earthly existence and what is my place in the Universe? Do we each possess the gift of Free Will and, if so, what is its purpose in the context of our Earthly sojourn? What is the nature of positive and negative energy? How may I become a better person/soul? Am I ultimately judged on a reward-punishment basis? Do universal laws exist which underpin the Universe and all of Creation? Is *karma* real and, if so, how does it operate and for what purpose? And what should be my relationship to Nature and the animal kingdom?

In *Transcendental Spirituality, Wisdom and Virtue: The Divine Virtues and Treasures of the Heart*, I identified 36 Divine Virtues which form the spiritual and ethical foundations common to all of the world's great religions and belief systems. The purposes of writing this book were to assist readers to identify with and elevate their own spirituality, to better understand their own religion or faith through a spiritual prism and to encourage them to understand and appreciate the spiritual and ethical unity of these religions. Throughout this book, spirituality was firmly anchored within a religious context. The sacred scriptures of these religions divulged a wealth of insights into God and God's attributes, Divine knowledge and understanding, the meaning and purpose of life on Earth and the various moral and ethical tenets we should aspire to live by in order to live a better and more wholesome life.

Upon completion of this book, and in furtherance of a long-held interest and fascination, my attention turned to examining the intriguing accounts of various and diverse people who had undergone a so-called "near death experience" and had written about their experiences and what they had learned and been told while outside their physical body. A treasure trove of material was located on the website of the International Association for Near-Death Studies (IANDS) containing hundreds of accounts written by such people. What they described in their written accounts included, but went well beyond, what can be found in the sacred scriptures. These accounts contained vivid descriptions of Heaven and the higher spiritual realms, what interconnectedness/oneness means, the nature and liberation of the soul-consciousness, the gift of Free Will and its purpose, the nature of soul agreements, the Universal Laws of Attraction, Reincarnation and Cause and Effect (*karma*), the nature of positive and negative energy, the significance of the death of our physical body and our post-physical death spiritual re-birth and life review. The study and collation of these accounts and the identification of common observations and insights drawn therefrom culminated in the writing of *Spiritual Revelations from Beyond the Veil: What Humanity Can Learn from the Near Death Experience.* Unlike the first book, this book decouples spirituality from a religious context. Indeed, numerous IANDS authors declared that before their near death experience, they had no religion and did not believe in the existence of God or an afterlife, while others who were followers of a particular religion or faith declared that after their experience, their particular religion was of less importance to them and henceforth aspired to be more spiritual in their outlook on life and in their dealings with others and the natural environment. The messages received from beyond the veil presented in this book are clear, compelling, easy to understand and life-changing. They dispel various illusions and delusions concerning death and the afterlife as well as the meaning of our earthly life which burden the human spirit and prevent us from progressing our soul's evolutionary journey and realizing ultimate liberation.

In this the final instalment of this spirituality trilogy, I examine the striking similarities and parallels in respect of the messaging to be found in the accounts of those who have written about their near death experience and that contained in the scriptural passages of the world's mainstream religions and belief systems. It would seem the eternal message has not changed; only humanity. This symmetrical and mutually reinforcing messaging is timeless in nature and operation and impervious to the ebb and flow of human thought and fashion. It is arguably more relevant today than in any previous period in human history as we continue to face increasing existential threats to the survival of humanity. In an era characterized by rampant materialism and consumerism, environmental exploitation and degradation, species extinction, global warming, cosmetic surgery, the so-called "selfie," a preoccupation with self rather than others, obsession with cell phones, the Internet, social media accounts, social influencers, media news feeds, "fake" news and so forth, it is perhaps timely to spark a revived interest in, and knowledge of, God and the afterlife and in seeking answers to the religious, spiritual, philosophical and existential questions mentioned above. An examination of these questions should preoccupy us more than they currently do, and at least be seriously pondered at some point in our lives.

For those who are terminally ill or fear the death of their physical body (or indeed life itself), for those who are grieving the loss of a loved one and for those who feel lost and confused about the meaning and purpose to their lives and what lies ahead of them, it is hoped that this trilogy of books will provide peace, comfort, assurance, guidance and nourishment for the soul.

Douglas Hodgson

Chapter 1

Introduction

What happens when we die? Is there an afterlife? And what form and description might that take? Does God exist? And is there a Heaven (or Heavens)? Do each of us have a soul or consciousness that survives the death of our physical body? Do each of us have a unique mission or assignment on Earth and what is the purpose of our existence here? Are we judged on a reward-punishment basis or are we assisted in a process of spiritual development through reflection and acknowledgment by higher beings from other realms? These are all fundamental metaphysical questions in the sense that they cannot be answered through objective study of material reality; they are largely beyond human sense perception, experience and understanding. Nevertheless, virtually all of us have a vested interest in the answers to at least some of these questions, although being caught up in the daily distractions and attractions of this world may draw us away from pondering these questions to the extent that perhaps we should.

Religions have developed over the millennia to assist in the answering of some of these questions and to provide a Divinely-inspired framework for ethical and moral conduct. They form an integral part of many people's lives. Whatever we conceive God to be and by whatever name we attribute to God, scripture reveals the mind of God and the essence of the Divine message or universal precepts, the Law, the Dharma, the Teaching, the Tao or the Way (as the case may be). It is through a reading and prayerful contemplation of religious scripture that God speaks to the heart of the believer, affording guidance, hope and comfort to the faithful. Various religions and belief systems – Baha'i, Buddhism, Christianity, Hinduism, Islam, Jainism, Judaism, Sikhism, Taoism and Zoroastrianism – have evolved from various common and unifying foundational spiritual principles and virtues. Certain Divine attributes and virtues are recognized and shared across this religious spectrum: unconditional love and kindness, compassion, charity and service, belief in one God (monotheism), the importance of prayer and its power, detachment from the material world and its delusions, courage, steadfastness in faith, gentleness, humility, living by the so-called "Golden Rule" (do unto others as you would have them do unto you), patience, peacefulness, purity, quietude, acknowledgment of wrongdoing and repentance, self-restraint (moderation), righteousness, simplicity, truthfulness, wisdom and understanding. These religions also either proscribe or caution against certain types of behavior: anger, greed, hatred, stealing, pride, over-indulgence, fault-finding, violence and killing, deceit and slander. Generally speaking, these religions recognize the eternal or immortal nature of the soul-consciousness which each of us possesses. They provide a means for the believer to become a better person and a pathway to salvation (or enlightenment/awakening/self-realization as the case may be).

However, for the past three centuries or so, scientific materialism and reductionism have postulated that only physical matter exists and that a separate consciousness cannot subsist outside the human body; consciousness exclusively depends on the functioning of the human brain and the body's physiology. This view has been widely and conventionally held and shared by the scientific and medical research communities. This consensus, however, is now being challenged and there is an emerging recognition within these communities that the human soul or consciousness survives the death of the physical body. The human brain does not create consciousness but is rather a mere filter of it. Such consciousness is eternal by nature. The so-called phenomenon of Near Death experience is consistent with such propositions.

Although accounts of such experiences date back to antiquity, they have only been systematically collected, documented and researched over the past 50 years or so by such eminent researchers as doctors Raymond Moody Jr., PhD, MD and Elisabeth Kübler-Ross, MD. Interest in this topic was reignited a decade ago when Eben Alexander, MD and neurosurgeon, published an account of his own near death experience in *Proof of Heaven: A Neurosurgeon's Journey into the Afterlife*. Hundreds of accounts or narratives of near death experiences written by those who have undergone them are to be found on the website of the International Association for Near Death Studies, Inc. (IANDS).

Near death experiences transcend time, ethnicities, cultures, geographical regions and religion. They have generally had a deeply profound and life-changing effect upon those who have had them. They involve persons who were resuscitated after having been pronounced clinically dead by medically qualified staff or who came very close to death without being pronounced clinically dead. The near death experience has had a particular impact on how those who have undergone them perceive more clearly how we are supposed to live our lives and what our purpose or mission is in the Earthly plane. They have also significantly altered their views on death and the afterlife, with the fear of physical death having left them. Many state that what they experienced was far different than a dream or hallucination and was more real than anything they have experienced in their Earthly life, being able to recall vividly and accurately what happened to them many years later. The spiritually transformative nature of the near death experience underscores the importance and value of core religious teachings on unconditional love, compassion, charity and service, and goodness.

Many of those who have undergone a near death experience use the term "ineffable" (inexpressible in words) or indescribable to explain their out-of-body experience and what they encountered. As one IANDS author has described, "It is not possible to convey the richness of my near death experience with words; it is a bit like trying to depict a magnificent sunset by drawing it in sand with a stick." This is due in part to the fact that human language and linguistics are just too impoverished to accurately and meaningfully describe the true nature of the afterlife or the so-called Ultimate Reality. Furthermore, their frame of reference is confined to their Earthbound experience and perceptive capabilities, and much of what they experienced in the other realms has no Earthly counterpart.

While some messages and concepts from beyond the veil appear beyond human comprehension and perhaps even beyond plausibility, many of the messages or revelations are deceptively and disarmingly clear and simple to comprehend. This latter category includes messages which are very similar to what is to be found in the sacred scriptures of the world's mainstream religions. It is these messages in particular in relation to which this book concentrates on, seeking to identify the striking and remarkable symmetry of the messaging reported on by the NDErs and that contained in religious scripture.

The book's format and methodological approach are as follows. Some 500 NDE accounts or narratives, written by those who have undergone a near death experience and which appear on the IANDS website, have been analyzed, with the focus being to identify common observations and themes which appear to emerge from these accounts. These observations have then been grouped together in a self-contained chapter to reflect a particular theme or topic. The accounts were all anonymously written and no identifying information has been included. Each dot point represents a separate account observation. As the reader will note, numerous observations and perceptions, while taken from separate accounts written by different authors, are strikingly similar and tend to corroborate one another through their frequency of repetition. Those observations and perceptions which were consistently repeated across the accounts and remarkably similar to each other form the bulk of the material presented in this book. Each chapter is introduced by a commentary section followed by the relevant NDE accounts which are juxtaposed with relevant scriptural references from various religions in order to illustrate the parallel nature of the respective messaging.

What then is the purpose of this book? First and foremost, this book aims to reveal to readers the mutually reinforcing, affirming and corroborating nature of the revelations brought back by NDErs from the Other Side and the fundamental messages and precepts contained in scripture representing diverse cultures, geographical regions and historical eras. It also seeks to provide comfort and assurance to those who have fear or uncertainty about the eventual demise of their physical bodies. It is to reassure them that their souls are created by God and are eternal and that there is a beautiful afterlife to be enjoyed within the higher spiritual realms (our true Home). It is to reveal that there is so much more to existence and reality than this life on Earth and our physical body. It is to reveal our purpose for being on Earth, one which is remarkably simple to comprehend although often difficult to achieve in practice. It is to reveal in a preliminary way observations and revelations on God, the Source and Creator, and Heaven(s), the interconnectedness of everything, and on universal metaphysical knowledge and understanding including various types of positive and negative energy. It is to provide validation and corroboration to those who have had a near death experience in relation to what they observed and learned while outside their body. And finally it is to reveal how our soul is a beautiful and eternal work-in-progress, evolving continuously towards communion with the Light.

Scriptural References
Hinduism

Virtue (spiritual treasures of the heart) alone will follow (the soul after death), wherever (the soul) may go, therefore do your duty (of obeying the sacred scriptures) unflinchingly.
(Vaisnava-Dharma-Sastra chapter 20 verses 39–53)

NDE Accounts

- Life on Earth is about loving relationships. All you can carry with you upon your physical death is the love you have given others.

- The love you give is yours for all eternity.

Chapter 2

God/The Source

Both the scriptures of the mainstream world religions and the accounts of those who have undergone a near death experience speak with one voice in their observations on, and understanding of, God/The Source as well as acknowledging and appreciating the ineffable nature of either trying to conceptualize or describe God. For example, in Hinduism it is acknowledged that God or Brahman cannot be defined or described in words or comprehended by the human mind. Nevertheless, God is perceived as pervading everything – the Ultimate, Eternal and unchanging Reality, the Universal Spirit, the Pure Consciousness and the Absolute, transcending this world and space, time and causation. The ancient *Sanskrit* name for God *Sat* (Existence/ State of Being/Reality)-*Chit* (Consciousness/Knowledge)- *Ananda* (Bliss) seeks to encapsulate some of the most important Divine or supra-human qualities.

That God is the one eternal, infinite, incorporeal, all-knowing and omnipresent bestower of all life and Creator of all that exists, is widely and generally shared between scripture and the NDE accounts which appear below, with a recognition or caveat that the essence of God can never be completely or accurately described and understood in terms or words, because human language is too impoverished and finite and our Earthbound experience much too limiting and restrictive to do justice to expressing the true nature of God. Nevertheless, both scripture and the NDE accounts have identified the following Divine qualities or attributes which are referenced in both the following scriptural passages as well as the relevant NDE accounts describing their encounters with God, the Light or the

7

Universal Consciousness and messages or revelations imparted to them by God or higher spiritual beings.

- God is the Creator and Sustainer of all life and all that exists, including the phenomenal world (Nature) in all of its diversity, and the absolute foundation of all things (including humanity, the spiritual realms, flora and fauna)
- God is the Light or Ultimate Reality
- God is a universal energy of Unconditional Love which permeates or runs through all things
- God is the immortal and eternal transcendent Supreme Being, without beginning and without end
- God is self-existent and self-subsistent (existing in and for Himself alone)
- God is incorporeal (a spiritual or nonmaterial/formless being)
- God is infinite (immeasurably great, unlimited, endless and innumerable)
- God is immanent (His continuing presence or Divine spark of Love is indwelling or within each individual)
- God is omnipresent (present everywhere and in all things at the same time/there is no place that God is not)
- God is All-Knowing or omniscient (knowing all things and having infinite knowledge of everything that has passed and everything that will be/nothing is, or can be, hidden from God)

Several of the NDE accounts state that we must give ourselves over completely to God in praise and love as we are His children and He our Father; our souls ultimately returning to God upon the demise of our physical body.

Scriptural References
Baha'i

My (God's) Eternity is My creation. I have created it for you. (Of Oneness: Words of Wisdom from the Supreme Pen of Baha'u'llah)

I have placed in you the essence of My Light. Therefore be illumined by it and seek no one else but Me.
(Of the Light: Words of Wisdom from the Supreme Pen of Baha'u'llah)

Your heart is My (God's) Home; purify it.
(Of Divine Humanity: Words of Wisdom from the Supreme Pen of Baha'u'llah)

Christianity

Be rich in prayer and love towards God.
(Luke chapter 12 verse 21)

The Kingdom of God is within you.
(Luke chapter 17 verse 21)

In the beginning was ... God.... All things were made by Him; and without Him was not any thing made that was made.
(John chapter 1 verses 1 and 3)

Everyone who does evil hates the Light, neither comes to the Light, but their deeds shall be reproved. But they who do (righteous deeds) come to the Light.
(John chapter 3 verses 20–1)

God is a spirit and they who worship Him must worship Him in spirit.
(John chapter 4 verse 24)

God is light.
(1 John chapter 1 verse 5)

How great is the love the Father has lavished on us, that we should be called children of God! And that is what we are!
(1 John chapter 3 verse 1)

God is love.
(1 John chapter 4 verse 8)

Submit yourselves ... to God.
(James chapter 4 verse 7)

Do you not know that you are the temple of God, and that the Spirit of God dwells within you?
(1 Corinthians chapter 3 verse 16)

Confucianism

There is only one Great Ultimate, yet each of the myriad things has been endowed with it and each in itself possesses the Great Ultimate ... which is not spatially conditioned; it has neither corporeal form nor body (the Divine attributes of immanence and omnipresence).
(Chu Hsi on the Great Ultimate: Chu tzu ch'uan-shu)

Hinduism

You (God) are the ... absolute foundation of all things.
(The Absolute Foundation of All Things: Bhagavad-Gita)

My (God's) shape is unmanifest, but I pervade the world.
(Everything is a Sacrifice to Me: Bhagavad-Gita chapter 9)

I (the Lord) am omnipresent as the stormwind which resides in space.
(Everything is a Sacrifice to Me: Bhagavad-Gita chapter 9)

The Great Soul ... exercises universal overlordship.... One God ... is the source of all.... Him Who is ... "incorporeal."
(The One God and the Phenomenal World: Svetasvatara Upanisad)

I am Brahman (God) (God is within me/the embodied soul and Brahman are an absolute oneness/the realization that Brahman dwells within each of us).
(Brihadaranyaka Upanisad 1.4.10)

If (those who make offerings) worship (Brahman) lovingly, they are in Me and I in them.
(Everything is a Sacrifice to Me: Bhagavad-Gita chapter 9)

Most humbly we bow to You, O Supreme Lord.... You are eternal, and beyond eternity.
(Artharva Veda)

O Almighty! You are the infinite!
(Ishawashya Upanisad)

Whoso loves and worships God, to God will that person come indeed.
(Bhakti and the Availability of God: Bhagavad-Gita chapter 7)

Islam

Remember God and God will remember you and be grateful to God.
(The Cow chapter 2 verse 152)

Truly, there is nothing hidden from God in the earth, nor in the heaven.
(The Family of Imran chapter 3 verse 5)

Not a leaf falls, but God knows it.
(The Cattle chapter 6 verse 59)

Allah is the Inner, Who is immanent in all things.
(The Heights (or The Wall with Elevations) chapter 7 verse 180;
Muhammad al-Madani The Ninety-Nine Most Beautiful Names
of Allah (No. 9))

Allah is al-Nur, the Light, illuminating both earth and heaven.
(The Heights (or The Wall with Elevations) chapter 7 verse 180;
Muhammad al-Madani The Ninety-Nine Most Beautiful Names
of Allah (No. 89))

God is the Creator of all things.
(The Thunder chapter 13 verse 16)

Verily, your Lord is the All-Knowing Creator.
(The Rock chapter 15 verse 88)

There is none in the heavens or on earth but shall return to the
Merciful God in submission.
(Mary chapter 19 verse 93)

God is the light of the heavens and of the earth.
(The Light chapter 24 verse 35)

God has knowledge of everything done by those who are in the
heavens and the earth.
(The Light chapter 24 verse 41)

God is the Creator of the heavens and the earth…. He both hears
and sees all.
(The Counsel chapter 42 verse 11)

Allah knows what the soul whispers and is nearer than the jugular vein.
(Qaf chapter 50 verse 16)

Allah knows all things.
(Iron chapter 57 verse 3)

He (Allah) it is Who created you.
(Cheating chapter 64 verses 2–3)

[Allah] is God the One, God the eternal.... No one is comparable to Him.
(Purity of Faith chapter 112 verses 1–4)

Jainism
The transcendent; its essence is without form (incorporeal).
(Acaranga Sutra: First Book Fifth Lecture Sixth Lesson Essence of the World: The Consciousness of Liberation)

Judaism
Love the Lord your God with all your heart and with all your soul and with all your strength.
(Deuteronomy chapter 6 verses 4–7)

The Lord is good; for His mercy, tender kindness and steadfast love endure forever.
(Jeremiah chapter 33 verse 11)

The Lord will be your everlasting light.
(Isaiah chapter 60 verse 20)

The Lord is my light and my salvation; whom shall I fear?
(Psalms chapter 27 verse 1)

It is a good thing to give thanks unto the Lord and to sing praises unto Your name, O most High.
(Psalms chapter 92 verse 1)

The Lord ... is ... plenteous in mercy and loving-kindness.
(Psalms chapter 103 verse 8)

The eyes of the Lord are in every place.
(Proverbs chapter 15 verse 3)

Judaeo-Christian Apocalyptic Literature

All things Thou (God) sees, and nothing can hide itself from Thee.
(The Book of Enoch chapter 9 verse 5)

His (God/The Lord of Spirits) compassion is great.
(The Book of Enoch chapter 50 verse 3)

Blessed be thou, O Lord ... of the whole creation ... all the heavens are Thy throne for ever.... You have made and You rule (over) all things.... You know and see and hear everything and there is nothing hidden from Thee.
(The Book of Enoch chapter 84 verses 2–3)

Fear not, for ... a bright light shall enlighten you.
(The Book of Enoch chapter 96 verse 3)

Sikhism

There is one God. He is the supreme Truth. He, the Creator, is.... Omnipresent, pervading the universe.
(Mul Mantra)

There is but one God ... the Creator ... immortal, unborn, self-existent, great and beneficent.
(God as Truth: Guru Nanak's Japji)

You (referring to God), O Formless One (incorporeal/of spirit).
(God as Truth: Guru Nanak's Japji)

I take the formless God into my heart and there make obeisance unto Him.
(From the Akal Ustat: Praise of the Immortal)

You, O God, the one Supreme Being, are fully contained in every heart and pervade everything.
(From the Rahiras: Guru Ram Das)

God is everywhere contained.
(God as Truth: Guru Nanak's Japji)

Utter not one disagreeable word, since the true Lord is in all.
(Granth Sahib: Hymn by Shaikh Farid)

O God, you are the true Creator. All creatures belong to you.... You are the totally infinite Supreme Being.... You are the same in every age.... You are the eternal Creator.
(From the Rahiras: Guru Ram Das)

The Lord ... gives life to all the world, His Light shines in all life born.
(Spiritual Marriage: The Bara Mah)

The One God is in every place.... He is in the soul and the soul is in Him.
(Hymn by Guru Arjan)

Taoism

It is unseen because it is colorless; it is unheard because it is soundless; when seeking to grasp it, it eludes one, because it is incorporeal.... It is called the transcendental.
(Lao Tzu, Tao Te Ching (In Praise of the Profound) chapter 14)

There is Being (the Tao or the Way) that is all-inclusive and that existed before Heaven and Earth. Calm, indeed, and incorporeal! It is alone and changeless. Everywhere it functions unhindered.
(Lao Tzu, Tao Te Ching (Describing the Mysterious) chapter 25)

Zoroastrianism

Ahura-Mazda (God), Heavenly, Holiest, Creator of the corporeal (material/physical) world, Peace!
(The Soul's Destination)

NDE Accounts

- My near death experience has left me with a profound certainty that God exists.
- God is the center and we are all spokes of the universal wheel.
- God told me that everything is all right and unfolding as it should.
- God's assurances are threefold: You are unconditionally loved beyond measure. Everything is always as it is supposed to be in the soul's journey. Everything will always be all right.

God as Creator

- God is our Creator and our soul returns to Him.
- God created us and dwells within us. To God we are all important and beautiful.

- The Universe was created out of love and we are all part of that Creation.
- Seek the Creator of all Creation who created you to find him. Desire to know your Creator and all things will be added unto you.

God as Infinity

- God is an entity of infinite loving energy without beginning or end; subsisting in every dimension, seen and unseen.
- God is never-ending infinity and love, contained in each and every thing.

God as Immanent

- God is within each of us and speaks to us within.
- Behold God in other people.
- God and eternity are within you.
- Eternity lies in the spiritual hearts of us all.
- God resides within us; within our heart, soul and spirit.
- God is immanent with His Creation but the creation is all a part of God.
- We are not God, but God is us.
- We are never separated from God.

God as Incorporeal (Light/Spirit)

- God has no form or embodiment. What could contain the Eternal?
- God is the Light and Energy permeating all of Creation and imbuing everything with being.
- The Light of God infuses the soul with the depth and breadth of eternal knowledge and the wisdom of the ages.
- The Light of God is peace, bliss, comfort, wisdom, joy, compassion and authority.

- The Light of God is absolute unconditional, ineffable love, acceptance and forgiveness.
- The Light is the manifestation of God's presence when He breathes.
- I understood that the intense glowing light was the presence of God.
- The Light is the heart of God.
- God = L.O.V.E. (Light, Oneness, Vibrations and Energy)
- God is Light and we are all children of the Light. We are truly never alone.
- The brilliant golden white light of Heaven is alive and has its own identity.
- Heavenly light is filled with love and acceptance.
- Heavenly light is of ineffable brightness and nature; a light of Truth and Understanding.

God as Omniscient

- The Light is all-knowingness and a peace that surpasses all human understanding.
- God is all-knowledge/omniscience.
- God knows everything about us and every thought that we have ever had. He knows our essence better than we know ourselves.

God as Omnipresent

- God is present within every energy particle of the Universe which is without beginning or end.
- God is everything and manifests in all energy.

God as Unconditional Love

- God is the energy of Love.
- We are all unconditionally loved by God.
- God loves us all so very much as we are all His children.

- All of us are children of God and loved by Our Creator beyond measure.
- We are all linked to one another as children of God by our Creator. Therefore, we must care for and serve one another.
- God is unconditional love beyond human words.
- God loves us just the way we are.
- God loves and cherishes as priceless each of us as we are; we must do the same towards others.
- God loves us beyond measure and wants us to trust Him with our earthly journey.
- We are all loved and cherished and never judged by the Creator.
- God is the energy of love that binds everything together and underpins all of the laws of physics.

The Path to God

- Peacefully surrender to God and your pain and anxiety will dissipate.
- Give yourself completely and consciously to the Almighty.
- Love and praise God.
- Cultivate a strong spiritual faith in God, the Source and the Highest Power.
- There is no one true religion or pathway to Heaven. Whatever speaks to our hearts individually is the best path for us. All paths lead us to the Source.
- Pray to the God of your heart rather than the one you have been taught by others. God does not condemn or punish but loves His creatures as they are, and helps them to become better versions of themselves.

Chapter 3

Heaven(s): A Glimpse Thereof

Most of us have pondered at some point in our lives what Heaven must be like or, indeed, whether Heaven exists at all beyond the realm of mythology. Such a place or concept is mentioned in the scriptures of most of the mainstream religions but, by and large, with some notable exceptions referenced below, is not described in any vivid or graphic detail. Some scriptural passages refer to Heaven in the singular tense, implying that there is only one Heaven; other scriptural passages refer to the plural "Heavens," indicating multiple Heavens. Some religions like Islam and Jainism, for example, refer to multiple or ascending or layered Heavens.

Many, but not all, of those who have undergone a near death experience do report that they found themselves in Heaven or at least at the threshold or boundary of Heaven from where they could get a close glimpse of what lay beyond the veil, the fence, the door, the archway, the stream, the pond or other forms of barrier between Earthly life and Heaven. The individual author descriptions of what they perceived do corroborate each other in many respects as will be come apparent in the following observations taken directly from the IANDS near death experience accounts. Those who report such experiences describe their frustration at not being able to fully, accurately and meaningfully describe what they perceived due to human language barriers and constraints posed by their limiting Earthbound experience. Their descriptive attempts, however, are multi-dimensional: Heaven can be considered a state of mind, an emotional experience (including joy, bliss and euphoria), a spiritual frame of reference in which negative energy or anything not of Unconditional Love and the Light is not permitted to enter, or a physical description by the soul's sense perception capacities (mostly vision and sound but not as these senses are experienced on Earth). Many authors of near death accounts note in some detail the radiantly beautiful unearthly colors of Heaven which appear to be alive and pulsating as well as Heavenly music which bears no Earthly counterpart. The descriptions of Heaven are circumscribed by the Divine attributes of unconditional love, acceptance, knowledge and understanding, peace, forgiveness and truth. Numerous accounts detail an intensely brilliant golden white Light which appears to have life and identity of its own. Other accounts refer to Heaven as our real home paralleling some scriptural passages referenced below which say that our souls return to God upon the death of our physical body.

Scriptural References
Baha'i
Remember Me (God) in My earth, that I may remember you in My Heaven.
(Of Divine Humanity: Words of Wisdom from the Supreme Pen of Baha'u'llah)

Days of blissful joy, of heavenly delight, are assuredly in store for you. Worlds, holy and spiritually glorious, will be unveiled to your eyes.
(Baha'u'llah)

[The] divine world is manifestly a world of light.
('Abdu'l-Baha)

Buddhism
(The Pure Land) is rich and prosperous, comfortable, fertile, delightful ... (it) emits many fragrant odours, it is rich in a great variety of flowers and fruits, adorned with jewel trees, which

are frequented by flocks of various birds with sweet voices ... these jewel trees have many colors ... there are nowhere any mountains but everywhere is even ... many kinds of rivers flow along calmly, their water is fragrant with manifold agreeable odours, in them there are bunches of flowers to which various jewels adhere, and they resound with various sweet sounds. And the sound which issues from these great rivers is as pleasant as that of a musical instrument emitting heavenly music. It is deep, commanding, distinct, clear, pleasant to the ear, touching the heart, delightful, sweet, and one never tires of hearing it ... the banks of those great rivers are lined with variously scented jewel trees, and from them bunches of flowers, leaves, and branches of all kinds hang down ... those rivers flow along, full of waters scented with the finest odours and covered with beautiful flowers, resounding with the sounds of many birds.

(A Vision of Paradise: Sukhavativyuha Sutra)

Christianity

Jesus said, "I thank thee, O Father, Lord of Heaven and earth."
(Matthew chapter 11 verse 25)

Whosoever ... shall humble themselves as this little child, they shall be greatest in the Kingdom of Heaven.
(Matthew chapter 18 verse 4)

In my (Heavenly) Father's house are many mansions.... I go to prepare a place for you.
(John chapter 14 verse 2)

I know of a man in Christ who fourteen years ago was caught up to the third heaven – whether in the body or out of the body I do not know, God knows.
(II Corinthians chapter 12 verse 2)

There came unto me (St. John) one of the seven angels ... (who) carried me away in the spirit and showed me the holy Jerusalem descending out of heaven from God, having the glory of God; and her light was like unto a stone most precious, clear as crystal ... the city was pure gold, like clear glass ... the street of the city was pure gold, like transparent glass ... the city had no need of the sun, neither of the moon, to shine in it, for the glory of God did lighten it ... there shall in no way enter into it any thing that defiles, neither whatsoever works abomination or makes a lie.... And (the angel) showed me a pure river of water of life, clear as crystal, proceeding out of the throne of God ... on either side of the river, was there the tree of life, which bare twelve manner of fruits and yielded her fruit every month; and the leaves of the tree were for the healing of the nations.... There shall be no night there (in Heaven), and they need no candle neither the light of the sun, for the Lord God gives them light.
(Revelation chapters 21–22 *passim*)

Hinduism

Place me in that deathless, undecaying world wherein the light of heaven is set.
(Rig Veda)

Islam

The truthful will benefit from their truthfulness. They will have gardens graced with flowing streams – their eternal Home.
(The Feast chapter 5 verse 119)

To God belongs the kingdom of the heavens and the earth.
(The Repentance chapter 9 verse 116)

God is the Lord of the heavens and the earth.
(Mary chapter 19 verse 65)

There is none in the heavens or on earth but shall return to the Merciful God in submission.
(Mary chapter 19 verse 93)

The servants of the Merciful God ... will be rewarded for their steadfastness with the highest abode in Paradise.
(The Discrimination chapter 25 verse 75)

He is God; there is no God but He ... to Him shall you (your soul) be returned.
(The Story chapter 28 verse 70)

God is the Creator of the heavens and the earth.
(The Counsel chapter 42 verse 11)

For those who are mindful of Allah, there are two gardens with shading branches and a pair of flowing springs with every kind of fruit.... There are two other gardens below these two of deepest green with a pair of gushing springs with fruits – date palms and pomegranate trees.
(The Lord of Mercy chapter 55 *passim*)

(The best of the believers) will enjoy Gardens of Bliss (wherein) everlasting youths will go round among them with cups of a pure drink that causes no headache or intoxication, there will be any fruit available that they choose.... They will hear no idle or sinful talk there, only clean and wholesome speech.... They will dwell amid thornless lote trees and clustered acacia with spreading shade, constantly flowing water and abundant fruits.
(That Which is Coming chapter 56 *passim*)

God has created the seven heavens one above another.
(The Kingdom chapter 67 verse 3)

Paradise contains a Garden whose soil is of the finest musk and saffron and ambergris, its stones of jacinths and jewels, its little pebbles and rubble are of gold, while on its banks are trees whose limbs hang down, whose branches are low, whose fruits are within easy reach, whose birds sing sweetly, whose colors shine brightly, whose flowers blossom in splendor, and from which comes a breeze (so delightful) as to reduce to insignificance all other delights.

(A Hadith from ibn Makhluf describing Paradise)

Jainism

Acquire (honor) through patience. You will rise to the upper regions (ascending heavens) after having left this body of clay.
(Uttaradhyayana: Third Lecture: The Four Requisites)

The spirits who are gifted with various virtues live one above the other (in ascending heavens), shining forth like the great luminaries and hoping never to descend (to Earth) thence.
(Uttaradhyayana: Third Lecture: The Four Requisites)

Judaism

In the beginning God created the heavens and the earth.
(Genesis 1:1)

Do not let your heart be hasty to utter any thing before God: for God is in Heaven and you are upon the earth.
(Ecclesiastes chapter 5 verse 2)

Thus says God, the Lord who created the heavens and stretched them out (and) who spread forth the earth.
(Isaiah chapter 42 verse 5)

Then (upon physical death) shall the dust return to the earth as it was: and the spirit shall return unto God who gave it.
(Ecclesiastes chapter 12 verse 7)

Judaeo-Christian Apocalyptic Literature

The winds in (my) vision bore me (Enoch) into heaven. And I went in till I drew nigh to a wall which is built of crystals and surrounded by tongues of fire.... And I drew nigh to a large house which was built of crystals: and the walls of the house were like a tessellated floor (made) of crystals, and its groundwork was of crystal.
(The Book of Enoch chapter 14 verses 8–10)

I (Enoch) saw all the secrets of the heavens, and how the Kingdom (of God) is divided, and how the actions of (humanity) are weighed in the balance. And there I saw the mansions of the holy.
(The Book of Enoch chapter 41 verses 1–2)

And it came to pass that my spirit ascended into the heavens and I saw the holy sons of God.... And the (archangel) Michael ... translated my spirit into the heaven of heavens, and I saw there as it were a structure built of crystals.
(The Book of Enoch chapter 71 verses 1–5)

Sikhism

They whom God awakens ... will find a home with comfort and peace in God's own palace.
(From the Sohila: Guru Arjan)

Taoism

(Humanity) is derived from nature, nature is derived from Heaven. Heaven is derived from Tao. Tao is self-derived (self-subsistent).
(Lao Tzu, Tao Te Ching (Describing the Mysterious) chapter 25)

Zoroastrianism

Excess (over-indulgence) encourages the most deadly sins and the soul so indulging will most assuredly be cut off from Heaven. (The Vision of Arda-Viraf)

NDE Accounts

- There is just not one Heaven; there are many levels to Heaven.
- Heaven is not a gated community; it is open to all.
- Our Earthly experiences are training us for the highest levels of Heaven.
- Heaven is a spiritual place but also a state of mind.
- Heaven is ineffable. It is more of an emotion. It cannot be described in words adequately.
- Heaven is peace and bliss that surpass all human understanding.
- Heaven is profound and expansive unconditional love, acceptance, joy, gratitude and understanding.
- Heaven is indescribable peace and total pure and unconditional love, acceptance and understanding of everything. Pain, fear and shame are unknown there. Heaven is love beyond comprehension.
- Heaven is complete and unconditional acceptance and understanding where fear, anger, resentment and self-blame have no place.
- Anger, hatred, aggression and fear are never permitted to enter Heaven.
- Heaven is our real home. It is joy, contentment, comfort, warmth and love. Earth life is a fleeting blip. When the soul returns home, it is as if it already knows this as its home and ultimate reality, but the soul forgets this on its return to Earthly life.
- Heaven is a sense of euphoria, perfect peace and of being home. No pain, wants or needs of any kind exist there.

- Heaven is a place of love, light and positive energy and an oasis for the replenishment of the soul after it has returned home from its mission on Earth.
- Heaven is the soul's real home; a place of happiness, contentment, warmth and love.
- The next thing I knew I was in a beautiful garden. I saw a female figure dressed in a long white robe. We were standing near a flower-covered arch. Everything was very peaceful. The woman told me that I was not allowed to pass through the arch because if I did I would not be able to return (to my earthly life).
- Heaven consists of rolling fields of unearthly intense green, trees, birds, blue sky, gentle warm breezes, crystal clear air and water, streams and soul-bodies in humanoid form.
- Heaven is bright and vibrant unearthly colors and sweet, clear and fragrant air with a gentle warm breeze. There may be found singing birds, streams, trees, grass and flowers; there may be heard unearthly music more beautiful than any other. Each of these emanates its own sound and vibrations.
- Heaven is light, sound, joy, bliss and harmony. All around me were beings of consciousness, of pulsing, colored light and indescribable music and singing filled with joy and praise for God and All That Is. Heaven is our home.
- Nothing can compare on Earth with the Heavenly music I heard, comprising rich sounds blended perfectly together as one. Its mesmerizing beauty was experienced with the entire soul as wind or a sound-wave.
- Heaven comprises radiant unearthly colors and buildings of luminescent glass crystal. They have apparent walls but their ceilings reach to eternity.
- Heavenly colors are alive, vibrant, glowing and pulsating.

- There is no sun in Heaven; only bright blue sky and intense light which is not harmful to the vision of the soul-body.
- Heavenly white light is alive, not hard on the eye, warm, welcoming and Home.
- The brightness of the Heavenly light did not hurt the eyes or cause them to squint. The focus remained sharp, clear and precise. I saw many beautiful flowers of unearthly colors.
- The beautiful, living and uplifting Heavenly Light had its own identity.
- The Light is indescribably brilliant, radiant and beautiful. It does not impair the soul's vision. The love which emanates from the Light is indescribable, having no Earthly counterpart. The Light is perfect understanding and love.
- I found myself in a place of great magnificent "light." It was so beautiful and felt so wonderful. I felt so much love. It was indescribable. This pure love I have never experienced on this earth. It was different from the light on earth. I did not feel heat like the sun's rays nor did I have to shield my "eyes" from its intensity.
- I was in a beautiful place. It was like a radiant, joyous landscape on a summer afternoon, but it was so much more – inexpressibly beautiful, serene and delightful with the most wonderful light pervading everything. Something like rolling hills with carpets of wildflowers. There were many beings there and they were blissfully happy. I was doing more than just seeing this; I was feeling it all with senses unimaginable. I knew these souls and they knew me. They radiated love and welcome. They were like family and we rejoiced in our reunion. It was rapturous. Although we didn't have physical bodies, we still "looked" the same, just more complete.

- I was in the most beautiful place I have ever seen. I was near a beautiful blue lake that was as smooth as glass except for two swans gliding through the water. At one end of the lake, a large willow tree leaned from the bank over the water. The grass was green and deep. The smell was that of a warm summer day, sweet and relaxing. Then I heard the music. It was music I have never heard before, beautiful and "angelic." I tried to distinguish the instruments, but I was unable to name them, and I realized the instruments did not have human names. Then the voices began, slowly at first, blending with the music until I could not distinguish the music from the voices. No voices spoke to me but my "soul" understood. The music and the voices were a lot like the wind in the trees, the kind of wind that soothes and caresses.

- I found myself in the most beautiful place. There was a large tree shading the most incredibly green grass surrounded by flowers of every color, size and shape that ever existed. I heard a humming sound like a tone of some kind. I became aware of the individual sound each flower made. It was like each flower was very much alive and had its own personality by the tone it made. All flowers together made a sound of perfection and harmony. I asked the Light in thought what was in the soil that would create such beautiful flowers. The Light answered "unconditional love." Every living thing, I was told, will find its own perfection with unconditional love.

Chapter 4

Faith and Hope versus Certainty of Knowledge

"Faith is the substance of things hoped for; the evidence of things not seen" (New Testament: Hebrews chapter 11 verses 1 and 3). Faith is belief in something which is not based on proof or which cannot be seen or perceived by the ordinary senses (sense-perception). It is a profoundly intuitive belief in the existence of something which cannot be proven objectively, scientifically or empirically.

In the religious and spiritual contexts, pure faith presupposes an absolute, constant, unqualified and unconditional genuine belief in the existence of, and trust in, God/Source, which admits of no doubt, questioning, wavering or exceptions. Such faith is based on a deeply personal and intimate relationship with the Divine. Faith resides in the human heart. In complete confidence, reliance and conviction, when we humbly petition God, we know our prayers have already been answered, perhaps not immediately or when we desire, but in God's time and in His manner (or, to put it otherwise, when our personal circumstances are ripe for receipt of the blessing). Although the petitioner or supplicant proposes, it is God Who disposes. Therefore, lean not unto your own understanding (Proverbs chapter 3 verse 5) but commit your burdens to God.

Faith is particularly important for us when difficult events or circumstances arise in our lives, including unforeseen events and circumstances caused by others. We earnestly search without success for an explanation or reason, but intuitively know deep down that nothing in the Universe is accidental, that everything which happens is for a reason or higher purpose and for our spiritual growth, and that all will ultimately be revealed, not in our time but in God's time, and that God is always with us and listening to us.

The NDE accounts which follow particularly emphasize that meaning and purpose can be found behind everything and that Earthly/human faith and trust in God are superseded in the higher spiritual realms by a certainty of knowledge and awareness of God's existence.

Scriptural References
Baha'i

Empty yourselves of doubts ... that you may be prepared for Eternal Life and ready to meet God.
(Of the Light: Words of Wisdom from the Supreme Pen of Baha'u'llah)

Humanity is ever degraded by ... lack of faith.
(Of Knowledge: Words of Wisdom from the Supreme Pen of Baha'u'llah)

Christianity

Ask and it shall be given you.... For every one who asks receives.
(Luke chapter 11 verses 9–10)

If you have faith the size of a mustard seed ... nothing will be impossible for you.
(Matthew chapter 17 verse 20)

Have faith in God.... Whatever things you desire, when you pray, believe that you will receive them and you shall have them.
(Mark chapter 11 verses 22–4)

Blessed are they who have not seen and yet have believed.
(John chapter 20 verse 29)

Your faith should not be based on the wisdom of (human philosophy), but in the power of God.
(1 Corinthians chapter 2 verse 5)

I live by faith, not by sight (sense-perception).
(2 Corinthians chapter 5 verse 7)

Faith is the substance of things hoped for, the evidence of things not seen.... Through faith we understand that the worlds were framed by the Word of God, so that things which are seen were not made of things which do appear (the material/physical realm was created by the unseen or incorporeal God).
(Hebrews chapter 11 verses 1 and 3)

Hinduism
Those of wisdom put their trust in God alone and resign (submit or surrender) themselves to God.
(Bhakti and the Availability of God: Bhagavad-Gita chapter 7)

Islam
Put your trust in God. God loves those who put their trust in Him.
(The Family of Imran chapter 3 verse 159)

God is our Lord and upon God believers put all their trust.
(The Repentance chapter 9 verse 51)

God is the Protector of those who believe.
(The Fighting chapter 47 verse 11)

God has written Faith in the hearts of the believers.
(The Wrangler chapter 58 verse 22)

Judaism

The righteous shall live by their faith.
(Habakkuk chapter 2 verse 4)

Trust in the Lord with all your heart and lean not unto your own understanding.
(Proverbs chapter 3 verse 5)

Whoso trusts in the Lord shall be safe.
(Proverbs chapter 29 verse 25)

I trust in God at all times.
(Psalms chapter 62 verse 8)

Sikhism

Exceedingly fortunate are those of God who have faith in Him and thirst for Him.
(From the Rahiras: Guru Ram Das)

Zoroastrianism

To attain God's friendship you must walk in His ways and place in Him the firmest reliance. The provisions (requisite for the journey to eternal life) must be faith and hope and the remembrance of your good works.
(The Vision of Arda-Viraf)

NDE Accounts

- In the higher realms, belief, faith and trust in God are superseded by a certainty of knowing, and awareness of, God.

- The knowingness and certainty I received from the infused universal knowledge while outside my body transcend hope and faith.
- As a result of my near-death experience, belief was replaced by knowingness and certainty.
- Hoping for something or having faith in something is not as reassuring as knowing it, as when you return from beyond the veil.
- All things happen for a reason; nothing is random in the Universe.
- Beauty comes of all things.
- Each life experience has a higher purpose and helps us to achieve our life's mission.
- There are no coincidences; everything happens for a reason.
- There is meaning in everything.
- Every trivial event has actual meaning and everything happens for a reason.
- There are meaning and purpose in everything.
- There is a reason for and behind everything.

Chapter 5

Oneness/Interconnectedness

On Earth we live in a dimension or realm of apparent separation and separateness. We perceive our world as full of separate physical/inanimate objects and people. Our reality is one of dualism in which the observer is separate or removed from what is being observed. Each of us considers that we are separate from every other human being. We are separate from the animal kingdom, from the chair we are sitting on, from the building we enter and the trees that surround us and give us shade. But is that really so? Is that the true or the ultimate reality?

In Chapter 2, one of the recorded observations of a particular near death experience stated that God is the energy of love that binds everything together and underpins all of the laws of physics. But what could that possibly mean or entail? The notion that in the physical or material realm each of us is not really separate from each other or the chair we sit on or an adjacent tree seems at first blush quite incredulous and fanciful. But the concept of Universal non-dualism or oneness is beginning to emerge from recent research in the field of sub-atomic quantum mechanics/physics. The notion of separation and separateness is a complete illusion. According to particle theory, every object or thing is connected with every other object through energy and its vibrations. Each particle is connected to every other particle at the deepest foundational level of the Universe. And in the spiritual realm at least, the perceiver and the perceived cannot be separated, being indistinguishable.

The NDE concept of interconnectedness/oneness has a religious counterpart to be found in the scriptures of some religions, including Baha'i, Hinduism, Sikhism and the

Abrahamic religions. They emphasize that God is One and immanent in the sense of dwelling within each individual and connecting all that is. God is also omnipresent in the sense of being everywhere and in all things at the same time. One of the fundamental tenets of Hinduism and Baha'i is the Unity of all created things. Underlying diversity there is unity, as all of Creation emanates from one and the same Source. All created life, including human, animal and plant life, is a Unity. Differences and distinctions may seem real in the Earthly plane but are illusory in the higher spiritual realms. And as numerous NDE descriptions documented in Chapter 2 observe, God is a universal energy permeating or running through all things and all of Creation.

From spiritual, religious and emerging scientific perspectives, each of us is intimately connected with everything in the Universe even though that does not seem real or apparent to us in the material/physical realm. As the NDE observations appearing below suggest, that everything is connected to and part of everything else appears to be far more readily apparent and appreciated in the higher spiritual realms.

Scriptural References
Baha'i

My (God's) Eternity is My creation. I have created it for you. My Oneness is My design. I have designed it for you; therefore clothe yourself with it.... O Dead Men ... you are drowned in the sea of polytheism while talking of Oneness. Oneness, in its true significance, means that God alone should be realized as the One Power which animates and dominates all things, which are but manifestations of its energy.
(Of Oneness: Words of Wisdom from the Supreme Pen of Baha'u'llah)

Purge thy mind of malice and ... enter the presence of Unity (oneness).
(Of Disputation and Fault-Finding: Words of Wisdom from the Supreme Pen of Baha'u'llah)

Christianity

You have one Father, who is in Heaven.
(Matthew chapter 23 verse 9)

God is one.
(Romans chapter 3 verse 30)

One God and Father of all, who is over all and through all and in all.
(Ephesians chapter 4 verse 6)

For there is one God.
(1 Timothy chapter 2 verse 5)

You believe that God is one; you do well.
(James chapter 2 verse 19)

Hinduism

All this that we see in the world is Brahman.
(Chandogya Upanisad 3.14.1)

One God is the source of all. Him who is without beginning and without end ... the Creator of all.
(Svetasvatara Upanisad)

The Great Soul ... exercises universal overlordship.... One God ... is the source of all.... Him Who is ... "incorporeal."
(The One God and the Phenomenal World: Svetasvatara Upanisad)

Meditate on the Supreme Lord of Love, be absorbed by Him, wake up from this dream of separateness.

(Svetasvatara Upanisad)

The experience of unity (oneness) is the fulfillment of human endeavors. The mysteries of life are revealed.

(Rig Veda)

He is One.... There is no Second God.

(Atharva Veda 13.5.20)

He is One. Come together, you all, with power of spirit, to the Lord of Heaven, who is only One.

(Sama Veda 372)

They know Truth who know that God is one.... He possesses the Supreme Power. He is One, the One alone. In Him all divine powers become the One Alone.

(Atharva Veda 13.5.14–21)

When a seer sees the brilliant Maker (Creator), Lord ... everything is reduced to unity (oneness).

(Maitri Upanisad chapter 6 verses 18–19)

Islam

There is no God save Allah.

(The Kalima or Creed of Islam)

Your God is one God. There is no god but He, the Merciful, the Compassionate.

(The Cow chapter 2 verse 163)

He is God; there is no god but He ... to Him shall you be returned.
(The Story chapter 28 verse 70)

God is the One and only God, the Eternal God. He begets none, and is not begotten. None is equal to Him.
(Unity chapter 112 verses 1–4)

Judaism

Hear, O Israel: The Lord our God is one Lord.
(Deuteronomy chapter 6 verse 4)

You shall have no other gods before Me.
(The Ten Commandments: Commandment No. 1 Exodus chapter 20 verse 3)

Before me no god was formed, nor shall there be any after me.
(Isaiah chapter 43 verse 10)

Thus says the Lord ... of hosts: "I am the first and I am the last; besides me there is no god."
(Isaiah chapter 44 verse 6)

I am the Lord, who made all things, who alone stretched out the heavens, who spread out the earth by myself.
(Isaiah chapter 44 verse 24)

I am the Lord, and there is no other.
(Isaiah chapter 45 verse 18)

Have we not all one Father? Has not one God created us?
(Malachi chapter 2 verse 10)

Sikhism

There is one God. He is the Supreme Truth. He, the Creator ... the Omnipresent, pervades the universe.
(Mul Mantra)

There is but one God ... the Creator ... immortal, unborn, self-existent, great and beneficent.
(God as Truth: Guru Nanak's Japji)

Thou, O God, the one Supreme Being, are fully contained in every heart and pervade everything.
(From the Rahiras: Guru Ram Das)

The One God is in every place.... He is in the soul and the soul is in Him.
(Hymn by Guru Arjan)

Taoism

The Tao (Way or the eternal and unchanging spirit or energy which permeates all life and matter) is unseen, empty, yet also profound and the creator of all that is.
(Lao Tzu, Tao Te Ching (The Meaning of Taoist Emptiness) chapter 4)

Complete harmony with the Tao means seeing the world as it is without distinctions (essential and inherent unity and interconnectedness).
(The Domain of Nothingness: Chuang Tzu)

Distinctions (based, for example, on wealth, power and fame) vanish in the Tao (the Way) and after death.
(The Great and the Small: Chuang Tzu)

NDE Accounts

- Everything is one. We are all connected.
- During my near death experience, I was shown how we are all part of God and how God is a part of each one of us.
- We are part of everything and everything is part of us.
- Energy is life – it all comes from the same Source. We are all One, everything is One, past, present and future.
- Everything is connected although we cannot perceive it in our physical bodies. Everything in the universe is connected to everything else. We are Source energy; the essence of God.
- Energy is the single common component which connects everyone and everything.
- Seek the Oneness of God. Separateness and duality are delusions of the Earthly realm.
- Experiencing the Oneness of God is like awakening from an earthly dream of separation and dualism and feeling a sense of returning Home to the Ultimate Reality.
- Humans dwell in a world of separation and separateness but God is One in and with everything.
- God is a spiritual unity, a oneness.
- God is present within every energy particle of the Universe.
- God manifests in all energy.
- We are all connected to all life. We are at one with all living beings.
- I know now that we are all connected on this earth, in a way that perhaps we do not understand but we are.
- I can't explain what ALL ONE is but I know that we are all one.
- I returned from my near-death experience with the feeling that we are very much all connected and that the only thing that matters is LOVE.

- Although the soul is separate, it is one with all things seen and unseen. Like an intricate web, the soul is one with all consciousness and the Divine.
- While in the spirit realm, there was never a feeling of being isolated or alone. I experienced being at one with ALL – never separate.
- In the higher realms, we are not separate from the universal consciousness.
- In the spiritual realm, all is interconnected.
- In the spiritual realm, the essence of every consciousness is simultaneously experienced.
- I ceased to be separate and my consciousness became one with the Light.
- Outside my physical body, there was a profound realization of never being alone and always being in communion with other spiritual beings.
- All souls are connected to the same Source, living different experiences.
- While outside my body, I experienced interconnectedness and oneness with everything in the universe.
- Outside of my body, I felt conscious but it wasn't part of my known Earthly reality. I felt such great peace. I had no sense of a body. It was just natural. It seemed like I was just floating around without any form in an expansive reality where everything is all connected. I was just part of everything. I didn't really have a sense of "me." I was everything and everything was me. There was just "one."
- We are all one river.
- All things there (in Heaven) are in Oneness.
- To understand everything, the soul must merge with, become absorbed into, and become one with, the Light.
- In the higher realms, the "I" or ego does not exist. There is no separation or dualism.

- In the Light, dualism becomes oneness. We become Love itself and our Earthly identity dissipates.
- We are all connected even though we erect barriers to separate, divide and protect us from our perceived and imagined fears and threats and to keep others from penetrating our lives. We are all linked to one another as children of God by our Creator. Therefore, we must care for and serve one another.
- We are one with everything; we are everything.
- We are all one in the universe.
- What is done to one is done to all. We are all one. Everything is one thing, made entirely of atoms. Things we can feel and touch are areas where the atoms are denser. It is not empty space between us but areas of less concentration of atoms.
- All things are connected to each other and every part of the Universe is important in its own way.

Chapter 6

The Ultimate Reality

Many believe in our contemporary secular world that what we cannot see or perceive with our five senses does not exist or cannot be considered to be real. Science and medicine are generally dismissive of the notion that our soul-consciousness survives the death of our human body on the basis that, in their respective views at least, consciousness depends exclusively on a functioning brain.

But many of those who have undergone a near death experience are adamant that their experience in the spirit world while outside their physical bodies was far more real than anything they have ever felt on Earth. They are now dismissive of the Earthly notion that only that which is physical or material and visible to the eye is real. They observe that our death in the physical Earthly plane re-births us into the spiritual realms which have been described by some of the authors as the "Ultimate Reality" in which the true nature of all things may be more readily recognized. Compared with this Ultimate Reality, our Earthly life is but a fleeting and passing dream. The death of our physical body is the leaving behind of our temporary home and a return to our real or true home in the spiritual realms. As we shall see below, there are scriptural passages which support these NDE observations. Hindus worship God or Brahman as the Ultimate/One Reality, the One Consciousness. This Ultimate Reality transcends space and time and is self-existent. It is the source of all knowledge – past, present and future – and encompasses everything.

Scriptural Passages
Christianity

That which is born of the flesh is flesh; and that which is born of the Spirit is spirit (the natural or physical realm only gives birth to things that are natural, but the spiritual realm gives birth to supernatural life).
(John chapter 3 verse 6)

Look not at the things which are seen (the earthly, physical or material world), but at the things which are not seen (the spiritual realm): for the things which are seen are temporal; but the things which are not seen are eternal.
(2 Corinthians chapter 4 verse 18)

The worlds were framed by the Word of God, so that things which are seen were not made of things which do appear (the material or physical realm was created by the unseen or incorporeal God).
(Hebrews chapter 11 verse 3)

Hinduism

O Brahma, lead us from the unreal to the real. O Brahma, lead us from darkness to light.
(Brhadaranyaka Upanisad 1.3.28)

Brahman is Reality, Knowledge, and Infinity.
(Taittiriya Upanisad 2.1.3.)

Brahman alone is real; the world is the appearance (Brahman is the only Truth; the world is unreal).
(Shankara, Vivekachudamani)

The world should be considered like a dream.
(The Teachings of Bhagavan Sri Ramana Maharshi: Who Am I?
(Nan Yar?))

Islam

The life of this world is but a sport and a play. It is the life to come (the Hereafter) that is the true (real) life, if they but knew it.
(The Spider chapter 29 verse 64)

Whatever you have been given is but a fleeting enjoyment for this worldly life, but that which is with God (Paradise) is better and more lasting for those who believe.
(The Counsel chapter 42 verse 36)

For those who do good in this world, there is good, but their home in the Hereafter is best.
(The Bee chapter 16 verse 30)

Taoism

Spirit is reality. At its heart is truth.
(Lao Tzu, Tao Te Ching (The Heart of Emptiness) chapter 21)

NDE Accounts

- Universal Consciousness – love, kindness and joy – is the ultimate reality; physical matter and the material world are insubstantial by comparison. Our souls have always been embedded within and cradled by it.
- Heaven is the soul's real home; a place of happiness, contentment, warmth and love. Earth life is a fleeting blip. When the soul returns home, it is as if it already knows this as its home and ultimate reality, but the soul forgets this on its return to Earthly life.
- The ultimate reality lies beyond this life.

- Earthly life is our dream; spirit is our reality.
- The spiritual realm is much more real than the physical realm, which is a transient illusion.
- You enjoy life in the earthly realm; super-life in the spiritual realms.
- Strive more for the spiritual and less for the material and physical.
- My near death experience was far more real than waking consciousness. This is so hard to explain. I was left with the conviction that a much greater reality exists for us beyond this world. I had seen it, been in it. What had happened to me was real, I mean really real, as if normal life is just an illusion in which we are immersed for our time here. Our Earthly reality is a wondrous, awesome creation, and it has a purpose, but a far greater reality exists.
- When we dream at night, we do not consider it real but consider Earthly life to be our reality. But Earthly life is not real and is but a dream compared to the spiritual realms.
- What we dream at night is less real than our Earthly life which in turn is less real than the Ultimate Reality to be experienced in the Higher Realms.
- This side of the veil is like a movie and when the movie ends you leave the theatre and enter into the real world. When you die, you similarly leave the physical world and enter the real (spiritual) world.
- My near death experience was similar to the feeling you have when you have been engrossed in a really good book for hours and then you put the book aside and notice the world around you. You had forgotten where you were and what time of day it was because the story held all your attention. You take a deep breath and notice the

real world, even as you reflect on what you have been reading. Life is like the book, and having put it aside I could see and reflect on the whole story, gaining greater perspective on the ultimate reality.

- I became aware that I was outside my body and I remember feeling with surprise and wonder that I had known this feeling before my life had begun, before I was born. I could feel my real self and this was joyous. I was looking down on my life and seeing how unimportant all the hassles were. I could see life as though it were a game I had been playing and how all the moves were just part of the game.
- Physical death is birth into the Ultimate Reality of the spiritual world which is more real than the earthly realm.
- Having shed my physical body, I felt more real than ever before. I learned how it feels to be truly alive as opposed to just existing.
- Death itself is painless. It is like going to sleep but you are still awake and alert. We are more alive after the death of our body than we are in this earthly plane.
- While outside my body, I never thought of myself as being "dead"; in fact, I felt more alive than ever. I was acutely aware of the Divine Presence, the Creator and spirit guides all around me.

Chapter 7

Beyond the Matrix of
Linear Time and Space

Most of us are accustomed to living our life according to linear beliefs and sequential patterns of existence. We believe that everything has a beginning, a middle and an end. Yesterday I enjoyed a game of tennis with my friend; today I am studying for my final examination which will be held tomorrow. In our human and Earthly experience, events follow sequentially one after another and our human history has thus been recorded.

But is this so in the higher spiritual realms and in Heaven? Linear time is an illusion of, and relative to, the Earthly plane although we consider it to be very real (and indeed seldom question it). The spiritual realms have little to do with the concept of linear time. According to the Hindu theory of creation, time is a manifestation of God. God is timeless, for time is relative and ceases to exist in the Absolute. The past, present and future coexist in God simultaneously. Buddhism emphasizes the so-called "Eternal Now." As a number of scriptural passages which are cited below suggest, a moment can seem like an eternity and an eternity like a moment in the higher realms. According to many of the NDE accounts (some of which are included below), linear time and space as they are conceptually understood and experienced on Earth do not exist in the higher spiritual realms.

Scriptural References
Buddhism

Do not pursue the past. Do not lose yourself in the future. The past no longer is. The future is yet to come. Looking very deeply at life as it is here and now, one dwells in stability and freedom. (Bhaddekaratta Sutta)

Give up what is before, give up what is behind, give up what is in the middle when you go to the other shore of existence (the spiritual realms).
(The Dhammapada chapter 24 (Thirst) verse 348)

Christianity

One day is with the Lord as a thousand years, and a thousand years as one day.
(2 Peter chapter 3 verse 8)

I am Alpha and Omega, the beginning and the end.
(Revelation chapter 21 verse 6)

Hinduism

The past, the present, the future – everything is just the word *Om*.
(Mandukya Upanisad)

I see no end to you, no middle, and no beginning – O universal Lord ... of all!
(Spoken by Arjuna: The Absolute Foundation of All Things: Bhagavad-Gita)

Judaism

For a thousand years in thy sight are but as yesterday when it is past.
(Psalms chapter 90 verse 4)

Judaeo-Christian Apocalyptic Literature

You (God) know all things before they come to pass.
(The Book of Enoch chapter 9 verse 11)

He (God/The Lord of Spirits) knows before the world was created what is for ever and what will be from generation unto generation.

(The Book of Enoch chapter 39 verse 11)

NDE Accounts

- The spiritual realm is non-linear. There is no past, no future, only the present. Yet the present includes the future and the past. Everything that ever happened or is ever going to happen is actually happening at that very moment.
- There is no such thing as linear time on the Other Side. Everything is always experienced in the now, including past and future.
- The spiritual realm is timeless. Time does not exist as we experience it on Earth.
- Time does not behave in the spiritual realms as we are accustomed to on Earth. It is not really one thing following after another; rather, a moment can seem like an eternity and an eternity like a moment.
- In the higher realms, each moment is simultaneously a second and an eternity.
- God's realm is a timeless, expansive and peaceful void.
- Time has no meaning in Heaven.
- In the higher realms, Time does not constrain our soul.
- In the higher spiritual dimensions, Time and Space do not restrict the soul as they do in the Earthly realm.
- There is no such thing as Time. It becomes non-linear in the spiritual world. It is only our human or earthly mind which makes Time linear. Your life – past, present and future – is happening simultaneously in the spiritual world.
- There is no past. There is no future. There is only now.

- There is no Time and Space. Everything simultaneously exists together in the higher realms.
- In the higher realms, the past, present and future (as we conceive them to be on Earth) are experienced simultaneously in a single moment.
- Every possible outcome for every possible situation is occurring at the same time, in the same instant.
- In the higher realms, you experience every possibility all at one instance.
- In the spiritual realm, the soul cannot sense Time. Time no longer limits or constrains.
- Higher realms are beyond the matrix of time and space.
- Time and space as we know these concepts on Earth do not apply in the higher dimensions.
- The concept of time is lost in the white light.
- I learned from the Light that time is meaningless in the higher realms.
- I was informed by my spirit guide that where I was, there were no time or space restrictions.
- Earthly time and space do not exist in the higher realms of spiritual existence.
- Time is only an illusion, made up to suit our Earthly experience.

Chapter 8

Positive Energy

The Universe and everything in it is energy which cannot be created or destroyed and which has always been, and always will be, moving in and through different forms and ever in transition. This is a Universal Law. God/Source is universal energy flowing through everything and making everything one. Universal energy is infinite and so can never be exhausted. Everything is made from the same vibrating universal energy which animates, connects and binds all things together. Everything is created from the same sub-atomic particles connected to Source energy.

Universal energy is infused into everything, including humans, animals, plants and trees. All living sentient beings are surrounded by their own energy auras. Energy intensity and vibrations vary between spiritual and physical matter (with the latter being lower). We are not our Earthly body; we are the energy that is one with that of God/Source. Upon physical death of the body, the energy merely changes form and the soul-consciousness experiences higher vibrations.

Humanity is subject to a continuous balance between positive and negative energy or what the Abrahamic religions (Judaism, Christianity and Islam) would term good and evil or what Hinduism, Jainism and Buddhism would refer to as wisdom/enlightenment/awakening and ignorance. Each soul manifests both positive and negative energy which finds its own equilibrium in the sense that positive energy attracts positive energy while negative energy attracts negative energy (see Chapter 10 concerning the Law of Attraction).

The types of positive energy identified by the authors of the NDE accounts comprise many of those qualities or attributes which mainstream religions identify as Divine virtues or attributes. These energies include first and foremost pure and unconditional love that transcends and persists regardless of circumstances. The love and light of God/Source are vibrational energies which flow through and connect all things. Other powerful positive energies include gratitude/thankfulness (a high-frequency energy), acceptance (of others and their flaws and one's circumstances) and forgiveness. While this listing is by no means intended to be exhaustive, other notable positive energies include joy, peace, kindness, empathy, compassion, serving and caring for others (without expecting anything in return) and mindfulness of God/Source. For those who actively pursue and live by the positive energy of the Universe, there is great reward.

The most powerful types of positive energies identified by both scripture and the NDE accounts are discussed below.

Unconditional Love and Kindness

Scriptural References
Baha'i
To love each other fully. To be kind to all people and to love them with a pure spirit.... All of our deeds must be done in kindness.
(The Commands of the Blessed Master Abdul-Baha)

The more we love each other, the nearer we shall be to God.
(The Commands of the Blessed Master Abdul-Baha)

In the world of existence there is no greater power than the power of love.
('Abdu'l-Baha)

Buddhism

Cultivate goodwill towards all beings. Let your thoughts of boundless love pervade the whole world.
(Sutta Nipata: Uragavagga, Mettasutta chapter 1.8.8 verse 149)

As rain falls equally on the just and unjust, do not burden your heart with judgments but rain your kindness equally on all.
(Buddhist teaching)

Christianity

You shall love ... your neighbor (others) as yourself.
(Luke chapter 10 verse 27)

Love your enemy.
(Matthew chapter 5 verse 44)

This is my commandment, that you love one another, as I have loved you.
(John chapter 15 verse 12)

Let us love one another, for love is of God; and every one who loves is born of God and knows God. Whosoever loves not knows not God, for God is love.
(1 John chapter 4 verses 7–8)

The fruit of the spirit is love, joy, peace, patience, kindness, goodness, faithfulness, gentleness, and self-control. Against such there is no law.
(Galatians chapter 5 verses 22–3)

Islam

[Show] kindness unto parents, and unto near kindred, and orphans, and the needy, and unto [your neighbor].
(The Women chapter 4 verse 36)

Judaism

The highest wisdom is loving-kindness.
(The Babylonian Talmud: Berakhot, 17A)

You shall love your neighbor as yourself.
(Leviticus chapter 19 verse 18)

Taoism

Those who seek immortality must ... be kind to all things.
(The Reward for Deeds: p'ao-p'u Tzu)

Compassionate towards yourself, you reconcile all beings in the world.
(Lao Tzu, Tao Te Ching (Three Treasures) chapter 67)

NDE Accounts

- The love you give is yours for all eternity.
- Life on Earth is about loving relationships. All you can carry with you upon your physical death is the love you have given others.
- The highest and purest form of Love is unconditional, radiating to all things living, unseen and inanimate.
- Love is the foundational core of everything that exists. Pure and perfect love is unconditional. It is not jealous or selfish and does not attach conditions to its flow.
- Unconditional love is a love for all that is, a love that does not differentiate and a love that exists everywhere, including within us.
- In answer to my question "What is beyond the Light?", the answer instantaneously formed in my consciousness that there are no limits or boundaries; Love is infinite.
- Unconditional love heals.
- Our purpose here is to discover unconditional love within ourselves and then offer it to others.

- Giving unconditional love to others is a blessing and returns to the giver an abundance of even more to give.
- Love everything and become one with it.
- Profoundly love all people without distinction and focus on the good in them. Put others first.
- The most important assignment in life is to love unconditionally, beginning with yourself.
- The Light told me to manifest Love, to live Love and to be Love.
- Be loving and kind in your thoughts, words and deeds. Be motivated by your soul heart.
- Loving-kindness towards others is a manifestation of the Light.
- Consciously evolve your soul by practicing love and kindness to all living beings and live in harmony with yourself and Nature.
- Earth is temporary. Love is the message of our earthly life.
- The most important thing in life is love.
- The only thing that matters is love. Petty stuff does not matter. What we consider important on Earth is not considered so in the higher realms.
- Material possessions do not matter; it is all about love for your fellow human beings and for God's creatures. The message I received is to love your neighbor, the needy, the homeless and those who do not know any better.
- Love is the ultimate answer to everything.
- The energy of love is the essence of life.
- Love is warm energy which penetrates the soul and heart.
- Love is a vibrational energy flowing through and connecting all things like an electrical current.
- Love is the most creative powerful force in existence.

- Unconditional love is a very, very powerful energy in itself.
- Once you experience unconditional love, you shall crave for nothing else. It is the most powerful force in the Universe created by God.
- All we need and can give in this earthly life is love.
- Love one another and be kind to each other.
- Cultivate a profound and boundless love and acceptance for others and all beings.
- The only thing that matters in your life is how loving your thoughts and actions are.
- We are here to love and be loved.
- The lesson is so simple. It's all about love. Understanding how much God loves us and how well we love ourselves and others.
- Perceive God in others and reflect that love back to them.
- I was asked (during my life review): "What have you done with your life? To what extent did you learn to love and assist others?"
- This life is a series of lessons and challenges to strengthen our spirits and expand our capacity for unconditional love.
- We reconnect with who we truly are and where our souls have come from through manifesting love and compassion towards others.
- We are here to do acts of kindness ungrudgingly and not expecting anything in return.
- Arguing and fighting are not what God intends for us. We are meant to try to be a good person and love and help each other.
- Small acts of kindness count for much in the higher spiritual realms.

Forgiveness and Acceptance

Scriptural References
Buddhism

If anyone should give you a blow with their hand, with a stick, or with a knife, you should abandon any retaliatory desires.
(Majjhima Nikaya chapter 21 verse 16)

Do not grieve over what is no more.
(The Dhammapada chapter 25 (The Bhikshu/Mendicant) verse 367)

Christianity

If anyone strikes you on the cheek, offer the other also.
(Luke chapter 6 verse 29)

Forgive and you shall be forgiven.
(Luke chapter 6 verse 37)

Confucianism

To be wronged is nothing unless you continue to remember it.
(Confucius)

Hinduism

Forgiveness.
(Saintly Virtue No. 22 of those endowed with a Divine Nature: Bhagavad-Gita chapter 16 verses 1–3)

Islam

God loves those who pardon others.
(The Family of Imran chapter 3 verse 134)

Show tolerance and forgiveness and enjoin what is good.
(The Heights (or The Wall with Elevations) chapter 7 verse 199)

Whoever forgives and makes reconciliation, their reward is with God.
(The Counsel chapter 42 verse 40)

Whosoever shows patience and forgives, that is a duty to God incumbent on all.
(The Counsel chapter 42 verse 43)

Do not grieve over things you fail to get.
(Iron chapter 57 verse 23)

Jainism

Whether it is life or death, whether gain or loss, whether defeat or victory, whether meeting or separation, whether friend or enemy, whether pleasure or pain, I have equanimity towards all.
(The Lay Person's Inner Voyage: Nityanaimittika-pathavali)

If beaten, a monk should not be angry; if abused, he should not fly into a passion; with a placid mind he should bear everything and not make a great noise.
(Sutrakrtanga: Book 1 Lecture 9: The Law)

Judaism

It is (a soul's) glory to pass over (forgive) a transgression.
(Proverbs chapter 19 verse 11)

Taoism

Though troubles arise the wise are not irritated.
Lao Tzu, Tao Te Ching (Self-Development) chapter 2)

Be content with what you have; rejoice in the way things are.
(Lao Tzu)

Zen Buddhism

When you forgive, you heal. When you let go, you grow.
(Zen proverb)

To find perfect composure in the midst of change is to find Nirvana.
(Shunryu Suzuki)

NDE Accounts

- Love all and forgive. This is the essence of our earthly life and learning.
- Our Earthly purpose is to learn and teach unconditional love, compassion and forgiveness.
- It is all about forgiveness.
- Forgiveness may be one of the most difficult things for us to do, but it is one of the greatest and noblest things we can ever do.
- My life review taught me that before we can let God's light and love in, we must forgive ourselves.
- Although I was having a hard time forgiving myself (during my life review), God had already forgiven me.
- Forgiveness heals the soul.
- Forgiveness is the best gift that we can give to ourselves. Lack of forgiveness poisons those who refuse to "let it go," and continues to affect our lives in a negative way until we do forgive. Forgiveness sets us free. If we choose to hang on to the hurts and resentments, we sentence ourselves to an existence based on fear not only in this life, but also in the next life you are given, and the next, until we learn. What matters is that we choose to free ourselves from the bondage that goes with the lack of forgiveness, lack of love, lack of mercy or lack of compassion.

- There is no fear, blame, judgment, pain or shame in the higher realms; only profound love, peace and unconditional acceptance.
- Empathy, understanding, forgiveness and acceptance allow the soul to progress to the higher realms.
- I could feel a magnetic pull and was being pulled into a white light. I wanted to get there as quickly as possible, because of all of these wonderful, ecstatic feelings emanating from the light: unconditional love, forgiveness, empathy, acceptance and deep understanding.
- Acceptance and forgiveness are the keys to Heaven.
- Everything in our life is fluid. Nothing remains the same. Every living thing grows and changes. Do not fear change. Accept change, let go and positive things will come your way.
- Love one another and accept others' flaws, and ponder their true potential.
- Accept others as they are rather than how we think they should be.
- Accept yourself for who you are but constantly strive to evolve into your Higher Self.
- After my near death experience, I felt for the first time ever a love and acceptance of myself and others.
- Accept the unacceptable and thereby embrace peace and calm.

Truth and Truthfulness

Scriptural References
Buddhism

They who imagine truth in untruth and see untruth in truth never arrive at the truth.

(The Dhammapada chapter 1 (The Twin-Verses) verse 11)

One who acts on truth and virtue is happy in this world and in the next.
(The Dhammapada chapter 13 (The World) verse 168)

Christianity

They who worship (God) must worship Him in spirit and in truth.
(John chapter 4 verse 24)

The Kingdom of God is within you.
(Luke chapter 17 verse 21)

Hinduism

Truthfulness.
(Saintly Virtue No. 11 of those endowed with a Divine Nature: Bhagavad-Gita chapter 16 verses 1–3)

Islam

Mix not truth with falsehood, nor conceal the truth.
(The Cow chapter 2 verse 42)

Do not say with your tongue what is not in your heart.
(The Family of Imran chapter 3 verse 167)

Assumptions can be of no avail against the Truth.
((Prophet) Jonah chapter 10 verse 36)

God is al-Haqq, the Truth.
(The Heights (or The Wall with Elevations) chapter 7 verse 180; Muhammad al-Madani The Ninety-Nine Most Beautiful Names of Allah: No. 18)

Jainism

Deceit is a passion which defiles the soul.
(Sutrakrtanga: Book 1 Sixth Lecture: Praise of Mahavira)

Judaism

Lying lips are abomination to the Lord: but they who deal truly (honestly) are His delight.
(Proverbs chapter 12 verse 22)

Judaeo-Christian Apocalyptic Literature

Woe to you who make deceitful and false measures.
(The Book of Enoch chapter 99 verse 12)

Sikhism

Truth is the nostrum (medicine) for all ills.
(Truth as the Heart of Conduct)

Zoroastrianism

Truth is best (of all that is good).
(Gathas 27:14)

NDE Accounts

- Search for the Truth. Your eternity is in your hands.
- The Truth lies within you.
- One's entire life (in the context of the soul's life review), including all of the good and bad deeds, are reflected upon in a clear and undistorted light. One's life cannot be misrepresented or lied about. Nothing can be concealed.
- Do not say in words what you do not think and feel in your heart.

Righteousness

Scriptural References
Buddhism

Overcome evil by good.
(The Dhammapada chapter 17 (Anger) verse 223)

The wise (person) who, as if holding a pair of scales, chooses what is good and avoids what is evil, is indeed a sage.
(The Dhammapada chapter 19 (The Just) verse 269)

Christianity

Blessed are they who hunger and thirst after righteousness: for they shall be filled.
(Matthew chapter 5 verse 6)

And the light shineth in darkness; and the darkness comprehended it not.
(John chapter 1 verse 5)

Everyone who does evil hates the Light.
(John chapter 3 verse 20)

Confucianism

When good is done, evil is corrected.
(The Investigation of the Mind: Wang Yang-ming's Conversations with Huang I-fang)

Islam

Whatsoever you do of good deeds, truly, God knows it well.
(The Cow chapter 2 verse 215)

Repel evil with good.
(The Story chapter 28 verse 54)

Repel evil with good and those who are your enemy will become your dearest friend.
(They are explained in detail chapter 41 verses 34–5)

Judaism

The Lord ... loves those who follow after righteousness.
(Proverbs chapter 15 verse 9)

He who pursues righteousness and kindness, will find life and honor.
(Proverbs chapter 21 verse 21)

Let justice roll down like waters, and righteousness like an ever-flowing stream.
(Amos chapter 5 verse 24)

Judaeo-Christian Apocalyptic Literature

Love uprightness and walk therein, and draw not nigh to uprightness with a double heart ... but walk in righteousness and it shall guide you on good paths.
(The Book of Enoch chapter 91 verses 3–4)

Taoism

True goodness is like water, in that it benefits everything and harms nothing. Like water it always seeks the lowest place, the place that all others avoid.... In generosity it is kind; in speech it is sincere.... Inasmuch as it is always peaceable it is never rebuked.
(Lao Tzu, Tao Te Ching (The Nature of Goodness) chapter 8)

The wise, trusting in goodness, always save others; for them there is no outcast. Trusting in goodness, the wise save all things, for there is nothing valueless for them.
(Lao Tzu, Tao Te Ching (The Function of Skill) chapter 27)

Zoroastrianism

Those who perform good works will have their reward in eternal life.

(The Vision of Arda-Viraf)

NDE Accounts

- I was asked during my life review what I had ever done in my life that was totally selfless? What kind words or deeds were spoken or done that were not motivated by the prospect of personal gain?
- The Being of Light asked me: "What actuated you? Did you act out of righteousness or because it was good for you personally?"
- Embrace righteousness and abhor evil.
- There is good and evil in each soul. Face towards the Light and turn your back on the darkness. The darkness cannot comprehend the Light.

Compassion and Empathy

Scriptural References
Baha'i

Under all circumstances, whether in adversity or comfort, in glory or affliction ... show forth love and compassion.

(Tablet of Baha'u'llah)

Buddhism

Accustomed long to contemplating love and compassion, I have forgotten all difference between myself and others.

(Milarepa)

Christianity

Rejoice with those who rejoice and weep with those who weep.

(Romans chapter 12 verse 15)

Be you all of one mind, having compassion for one another, love one another.
(1 Peter chapter 3 verse 8)

Confucianism
The feeling of distress (at witnessing the suffering of others) is the beginning of humaneness (compassion).
(The Innateness of the Four Great Virtues: Mencius)

Hinduism
Compassion towards all living beings.
(Saintly Virtue No. 16 of those endowed with a Divine Nature: Bhagavad-Gita chapter 16 verses 1–3)

Islam
Allah is al-Rahim, the Compassionate, who is gentle and full of compassion.
(The Heights (or The Wall with Elevations) chapter 7 verse 180; Muhammad al-Madani The Ninety-Nine Most Beautiful Names of Allah: No. 30)

Judaism
Show mercy and compassion to all.
(Zechariah chapter 7 verse 9)

If your enemy is hungry, give them bread to eat; if thirsty, give them water to drink.
(Proverbs chapter 25 verse 21)

Taoism
Tao (the Way) has three treasures which one must guard and cherish. The first is called compassion.
(Lao Tzu, Tao Te Ching (Three Treasures) chapter 67)

Those who seek immortality must ... rejoice in the fortune of others and pity their suffering.
(The Reward for Deeds: p'ao-p'u Tzu)

Zen Buddhism

Working with deep compassion for all sentient beings.... This is what is called Buddha. Do not search beyond it.
(Zen Master Dogen)

NDE Accounts

- We must love the unlovable. We must see others and their struggles through the eyes of God. Empathy begets compassion.
- Manifest love and compassion towards every living thing. Feel what they are feeling; manifest empathy.
- Be more empathetic and less judgmental.
- Empathize with the thoughts and feelings and circumstances of others.
- Manifest your compassion outwardly to others.
- Become the essence of compassion.
- I learned (from my life review) that our actions and words are powerful and possess rippling and lasting consequences. Therefore, we must empathize with others around us who may be affected before we speak and act.
- What changed for me as a result of my near death experience? I now feel people's emotions as though they are inside me. I now have reliable intuition.
- After my near death experience, I am attuned to healing energies and intuitively feel the feelings of others.

Material and Spiritual Charity

Scriptural References
Baha'i
Charity is beloved and acceptable before God and is accounted the chief among all good deeds.
(Tablet of Baha'u'llah: Words of Paradise)

Buddhism
Giving is the noble expression of the benevolence of the mighty.
(Jatakamala chapter 3 verse 23)

Christianity
Give your alms in secret: and your Father (in Heaven) Who sees in secret shall reward you openly.
(Matthew chapter 6 verse 4)

Let no one seek their own good, but the good of their neighbor.
(1 Corinthians chapter 10 verse 24)

Hinduism
Charity.
(Saintly Virtue No. 4 of those endowed with a Divine Nature: Bhagavad-Gita chapter 16 verses 1–3)

Islam
Whatever alms you give shall benefit your soul, provided that you give them for the love of God. And whatever alms you give shall be repaid to you in full.
(The Cow chapter 2 verse 272)

Judaism

There are those who divest themselves (provide alms) for others and yet increase (in spiritual treasures of the heart and soul): and there are those who withhold (from their possessions) more than is meet (appropriate), but it tends to (spiritual) poverty.
(Proverbs chapter 11 verse 24)

Those who have pity on the poor (draw closer to) the Lord: and what has been given will be repaid.
(Proverbs chapter 19 verse 17)

Sikhism

Charity, almsgiving and prayer are the knowledge of eternity that is the Lord.
(Spiritual Marriage: The Bara Mah)

Taoism

Those who seek immortality must ... relieve the destitute and save the poor.
(The Reward for Deeds: p'ao-p'u Tzu)

Having given to others freely, (the wise person) will have in plenty (those who are generous and charitable towards others will be rewarded with abundant blessings and security).
(Lao Tzu, Tao Te Ching (The Nature of the Essential) chapter 81)

Zen Buddhism

That which you give to another will become your own sustenance; if you light a lamp for another, your own way will be lit.
(Nichiren)

Zoroastrianism

(Spiritual riches) shall be given to those who work in this world for Ahura-Mazda (God) and wield according to the will of Ahura the power He gave to them to relieve the poor.
(Prayer of Ahuna Vairya)

NDE Accounts

- Make sure you give more than you take.
- We exist on this earthly plane to struggle, to learn, to live our life to the full, to spiritually evolve, to serve God, to assist other souls in their spiritual evolution and to add something of value to the world.
- The more we help others, the better will be our soul journey.
- It is the selfless things we do for others out of unconditional love that really matter.

Simplicity/Innocence

Scriptural References
Christianity

Except you ... become as little children, you shall not enter the Kingdom of Heaven. Whosoever shall humble (oneself) as this little child, the same is greatest in the Kingdom of Heaven.
(Matthew chapter 18 verses 3–4)

Taoism

By close attention to the will, compelling gentleness, one can become like a little child.
(Lao Tzu, Tao Te Ching (What Is Possible) chapter 10)

They who (understand themselves) ... will come again to the nature of a little child. They who know their innocence and

recognize their sin can become the world's model. Being a world's model, infinite *teh* (virtue) will not fail, they will return to the Absolute. They who know the glory of their nature and recognize also their limitations ... will revert to simplicity.
(Lao Tzu, Tao Te Ching (Returning to Simplicity) chapter 28)

Zen Buddhism

Zen is to have the heart and soul of a little child.
(Takuan Soho)

NDE Accounts

- Be simple and childlike.
- Everything that truly matters – love, joy, truth and honesty – are to be found in the smiling eyes and face of an innocent child.
- It is a blessing to approach the end of our life on Earth with the innocence, love, joy and spontaneity of a young child.

Spiritual Fortitude

Scriptural References
Buddhism

The wise make for themselves an island that no flood can overwhelm.
(The Dhammapada chapter 2 (On Earnestness) verse 25)

Christianity

Always pray and never give up.
(Luke chapter 18 verse 1)

Whenever you have to face trials of many kinds, consider yourself supremely happy, in the knowledge that such testing ... breeds fortitude.
(James chapter 1 verses 2–3)

Hinduism

Steadfastness in spiritual knowledge.
(Saintly Virtue No. 3 of those endowed with a Divine Nature:
Bhagavad-Gita chapter 16 verses 1–3)

Islam

The righteous are those who are steadfast in prayer and in times
of misfortune and adversity.
(The Cow chapter 2 verse 177)

Verily, along with every hardship is relief.
(The Opening Forth chapter 94 verse 5)

Judaism

The righteous fall seven times and rise up again.
(Proverbs chapter 24 verse 16)

Zoroastrianism

Without trouble nothing can be attained.
(The Vision of Arda-Viraf)

NDE Accounts

- Struggle and pain are not to be feared; rather, they are opportunities for the soul to learn, grow and evolve.
- The meaning of life is to struggle and through that struggle to learn. Life is the teacher; our classroom is our experiences.
- Regardless of the struggles and challenges we face in life, they are temporary and fleeting but necessary for the evolution of the soul-consciousness.
- Life is replete with struggles and challenges, but that is the way it is supposed to be; to enable us to learn and persevere.
- Suffering allows us to overcome and grow.

- Through pain and suffering come greatness and nobility (of the spirit).
- Emotions, worries and challenges are part of our earthly journey.
- The lot of humans is to experience the full range of emotions so that we may feel our earthly journey and better learn and grow from it.
- Persevere until the end.

Joy and Gratitude

Scriptural References
Baha'i

Be thankful to Me (God).
(Of Divine Humanity: Words of Wisdom from the Supreme Pen of Baha'u'llah)

Christianity

Ask and you shall receive, that your joy may be full.
(John chapter 16 verse 24)

In everything by prayer and supplication with thanksgiving let your requests be made known unto God.
(Philippians chapter 4 verse 6)

Islam

Remember God and God will remember you and be grateful to God.
(The Cow chapter 2 verse 152)

God will reward the grateful.
(The Family of Imran chapter 3 verse 144)

God is full of grace for humanity, but most ... do not give thanks.
(The Ants chapter 27 verse 73)

Judaism
It is a good thing to give thanks unto the Lord and to sing praises unto Your name, O most High.
(Psalms chapter 92 verses 1–2)

Zoroastrianism
God ... requires only two things of humanity: the first, that they should not sin: the next, that they shall be grateful of the many blessings He is continually bestowing upon them.
(The Vision of Arda-Viraf)

NDE Accounts
- Feel love, joy and gratitude to attract positive energy into your life.
- Create joy for yourselves and others. You are meant to have and deserve happiness.
- Experience joy, peace and calmness.
- We are here to explore, experience and find joy in our earthly existence.
- Be exceedingly thankful for the countless blessings God has conferred upon you. Joy and gratitude are two of the highest vibrational states.
- Be grateful for your life, soul, breath and all that sustains you.
- Be grateful for your Earthly life and respect it.
- There is so much to be grateful for and joyful about if we set aside the time to reflect thereon.
- Be grateful for the things you have rather than complain about what you don't have. When you focus on what you don't have, you will attract more of what you don't have into your life. Focus on what brings you joy and gratitude.

Chapter 9

Negative Energy

As we have seen in Chapter 5 and the previous chapter, the Earthly plane of existence is characterized by duality in which the observer and the observed are separate and everything exists in a continuous and dynamic balance between positive and negative energy or what the Abrahamic religions (Judaism, Christianity and Islam) term good and evil or what Eastern religions such as Buddhism, Hinduism and Jainism refer to as wisdom or enlightenment/awakening and ignorance. Each soul-consciousness simultaneously manifests both positive and negative energy which finds its own equilibrium, with positive energy attracting positive energy and negative energy attracting negative energy (see the next chapter for an explanation of the Universal Law of Attraction).

While positive energy comprises many of those qualities which mainstream religions attribute as Divine virtues, negative energy is not of God and does not exist in the higher spiritual realms. As one IANDS author observes, God is not about fear, condemnation or judgment. Humanity and religion have used God to facilitate human control and to instill fear of judgment and condemnation into humans and to shape their beliefs. But negative thoughts and emotions and substance abuse alter our soul's energy in the Earthly plane. As like attracts like, the manifestation of negative thoughts and deeds will surely be returned to us by the Universe. The killing or harming of other beings is self-harm. Being judgmental, biased and discriminatory towards others also lessens our energy flow and harms our soul. Anger, greed, selfishness, guilt, worry and anxiety are other types of negative energy which alter our soul's energy intensity and vibrations and impede the Light of God from flowing freely within and through us. Illnesses and diseases begin on an energetic level before they manifest physically and are produced by fear. Only the universal energy of unconditional love can eradicate fear and thereby heal the body. There is no fear in love; but perfect love casts out fear (1 John chapter 4 verse 18).

Life is a precious gift from God/Source which should not be prematurely terminated. It is exclusively the Divine prerogative to end physical life. Killing ourselves and others interferes with and frustrates God's purpose for those lives. Those who have undergone a near death experience after having unsuccessfully attempted to end their own life report that this is against the universal laws, as we should not attempt to release ourselves from our pre-physical birth soul agreement prematurely, having left our life's mission and purpose, however modest they may be, unfulfilled.

What follows is a representative sample of observations made on negative energy by those who have undergone an NDE and those scriptural references which corroborate or parallel these observations and insights.

Scriptural References
Baha'i

Purge thy mind of malice and ... enter the presence of Unity.
(Of Disputation and Fault-Finding: Words of Wisdom from the Supreme Pen of Baha'u'llah)

Why have you overlooked your own faults and are observing defects in My servants?... Breathe not the sins of any one as long as you are a sinner. If you do contrary to this command, you are not of Me.
(On Disputation and Fault-Finding: Words of Wisdom from the Supreme Pen of Baha'u'llah)

To be silent concerning the faults of others; to pray for them; and help them, through kindness, to correct their faults. To look always at the good and not at the bad.... To never allow ourselves to speak one unkind word about another; even though that other be our enemy.
(The Commands of the Blessed Master Abdul-Baha)

Think not the faults of others to be great, that your own may not seem great.
(On Disputation and Fault-Finding: Words of Wisdom from the Supreme Pen of Baha'u'llah)

Buddhism

Hatred does not cease in this world by hatred: hatred ceases by love; this is an eternal truth.
(The Dhammapada chapter 1 (The Twin-Verses) verse 5)

Many do not know we are here in this world to live in harmony. Those who know this do not fight against each other.
(The Dhammapada chapter 1 (The Twin-Verses) verse 6)

Overcome anger by love.
(The Dhammapada chapter 17 (Anger) verse 223)

Riches make most people greedy. Any possession that increases the sin of selfishness ... is nothing but a drawback in disguise.
(Jatakamala chapter 5 verses 5 and 15)

Verily, it is the law of humanity that though one accumulates hundreds of thousands of worldly goods, one still succumbs to the spell of death.
(Udanavarga chapter 1 verses 20–1)

I rejoice free from fear.
(Majjhima Nikaya chapter 92 verses 17 and 19)

The faults of others are easier to see than one's own.
(Udanavarga chapter 27 verse 1)

One should not dwell on the faults of others, into things done and left undone by others. One should rather consider what by oneself is done and left undone.
(The Dhammapada chapter 4 (Flowers) verse 50)

Abstain from taking life. Do not kill anything that lives/has the life-force.
(First Basic Precept: The Five Precepts and their Meaning: Buddhagosa's Commentary: Papanasudani)

All tremble at punishment; all fear death. Remember that you are like them, therefore one should not kill, nor cause to slaughter.
(The Dhammapada chapter 10 (Punishment) verse 129)

Do not grieve over what is no more.
(The Dhammapada chapter 25 (The Bhikshu/Mendicant) verse 367)

Christianity

Let everyone be swift to hear, slow to speak and slow to wrath.
(James chapter 1 verse 19)

Love your enemies, bless them who curse you, do good to them who hate you and pray for them who despitefully (maliciously) use you and persecute you. That you may be children of your

Father ... in Heaven: for He makes His sun to rise on the evil and on the good and sends rain on the just and on the unjust.
(Matthew chapter 5 verses 44–5)

Love your enemies, do good to those who hate you.
(Luke chapter 6 verse 27)

Take heed and beware of covetousness; for a person's life (richness of the soul) consists not in the abundance of (worldly) things which are possessed.
(Luke chapter 12 verse 15)

Do not lay up for yourselves treasures upon earth, where moth and rust corrupt and where thieves break through and steal. But lay up for yourselves treasures in heaven, where neither moth nor rust corrupt and where thieves do not break through nor steal. For where your treasure is, there will your heart be also.
(Matthew chapter 6 verses 19–21)

Be without covetousness and be content with such things as you have.
(Hebrews chapter 13 verse 5)

Which of you by taking thought (worry or anxiety) can add one cubit unto one's stature?
(Matthew chapter 6 verse 27)

Take no thought about what we shall eat or what we shall drink or what clothes we shall wear.... But seek first the kingdom of God and His righteousness; and all these things shall be added unto you. Take therefore no thought for tomorrow, for tomorrow shall have worries of its own. Sufficient for each day is its own trouble.
(Matthew chapter 6 verses 31, 33–34)

Let not your heart be troubled, neither let it be afraid.
(John chapter 14 verse 27)

There is no fear in love; but perfect love casts out fear.... One who fears is not made perfect in love.
(1 John chapter 4 verse 18)

Those who are without sin, let them cast the first stone.
(John chapter 8 verse 7)

Judge not and you shall not be judged: condemn not and you shall not be condemned.
(Luke chapter 6 verse 37)

Judge not, that you be not judged. For with what judgment you judge, you shall be judged: and with what measure you mete, it shall be measured to you again. And why do you behold the mote (speck) that is in your (neighbor's) eye, but consider not the beam that is in your own eye?
(Matthew chapter 7 verses 1–3)

Those who live by the sword shall die by the sword.
(Matthew chapter 26 verse 52)

You shall not murder.
(Romans chapter 13 verse 9)

Hinduism

Absence of anger.
(Saintly Virtue No. 12 of those endowed with a Divine Nature: Bhagavad-Gita chapter 16 verses 1–3)

Against an angry person do not in return show anger, bless when you are cursed.
(The Laws of Manu: Manava-dharma-sastra chapter 6 verses 33–60)

By the restraint of (one's) senses, by the destruction of ... hatred and by the abstention from injuring...creatures, (one) becomes fit for immortality.
(The Laws of Manu: Manava-dharma-sastra chapter 6 verses 33–60)

Bearing enmity towards none.
(Saintly Virtue No. 25 of those endowed with a Divine Nature: Bhagavad-Gita chapter 16 verses 1–3)

Absence of covetousness.
(Saintly Virtue No. 17 of those endowed with a Divine Nature: Bhagavad-Gita chapter 16 verses 1–3)

Fearlessness.
(Saintly Virtue No. 1 of those endowed with a Divine Nature: Bhagavad-Gita chapter 16 verses 1–3)

Restraint from fault-finding.
(Saintly Virtue No. 15 of those endowed with a Divine Nature: Bhagavad-Gita chapter 16 verses 1–3)

Non-violence.
(Saintly Virtue No. 10 of those endowed with a Divine Nature: Bhagavad-Gita chapter 16 verses 1–3)

To kill means to separate the soul from the body.
(Ramanuja on the *Atman* and Body: Commentary to the Bhagavad-Gita)

The mind should not be allowed to wander towards ... what concerns other people. However bad other people may be, one should bear no hatred for them ... hatred should be eschewed. All that one gives to others one gives to one's self.
(The Teachings of Bhagavan Sri Ramana Maharshi: Who Am I? (Nan Yar?))

Whatever burdens are thrown on God, He bears them. Since the supreme power of God makes all things move, why should we ... constantly worry ourselves with thoughts as to what should be done and how, and what should not be done and how not? We know that the train carries all loads, so after getting on it why should we carry our small luggage on our head to our discomfort, instead of putting it down in the train and feeling at ease?
(The Teachings of Bhagavan Sri Ramana Maharshi: Who Am I? (Nan Yar?))

Islam

Those who ... restrain their anger and pardon others ... God loves.
(The Family of Imran chapter 3 verse 134)

Humanity covets ... gold and silver. This is the pleasure of the present world's life, but God has the excellent return (Paradise) with Him.
(The Family of Imran chapter 3 verse 14)

Souls are prone to greed. But if you act kindly and fear (are mindful of) God ... know that God is aware of all your actions.
(The Women chapter 4 verse 128)

Those who are saved from their own covetousness, they are the prosperous (spiritually enlightened).
(Cheating chapter 64 verse 16)

Nothing shall befall us but what God has prescribed for us; He is our Lord; in God let the believers put all their trust.
(The Repentance chapter 9 verse 51)

Do not kill yourselves.
(The Women chapter 4 verse 29)

If anyone killed a person ... it would be as if they killed all (humanity) and if anyone saved a life, it would be as if they saved the life of all (humanity).
(The Table chapter 5 verse 32)

Jainism

Wrath is a passion which defiles the soul.
(Sutrakrtanga (Praise of Mahavira) Book 1 Sixth Lecture)

Greed is a passion which defiles the soul.
(Sutrakrtanga (Praise of Mahavira) Book 1 Sixth Lecture)

Forgetting that life will have an end, the rash and foolish are full of selfishness; they toil day and night, greedy of wealth, as if they never grow old or die.
(Sutrakrtanga (Carefulness) Book 1 Tenth Lecture)

Look at all people with an impartial mind.
(Sutrakrtanga (Carefulness) Book 1 Tenth Lecture)

I renounce all killing of living beings.... Nor shall I myself kill living beings (nor cause others to do it, nor consent to it).
(First Great Vow: Acaranga Sutra)

Having heard (the eternal law) humans will ... abstain from killing living beings.
(Uttaradhyayana: Third Lecture: The Four Requisites)

All breathing, existing, living, sentient creatures should not be slain, nor treated with violence, nor abused, nor tormented. This is the pure, unchangeable, eternal law.
(Acaranga Sutra: Fourth Lecture: Righteousness)

Those who guard their soul and subdue their senses should never assent to anybody killing living beings.
(Sutrakrtanga: Book 1 Eleventh Lecture: The Path)

One should do no harm to anybody, neither by thoughts, nor words, nor acts.
(Sutrakrtanga: Book 1 Eleventh Lecture: The Path)

This is the quintessence of wisdom: not to kill anything.... One should cease to injure living beings.... For this has been called the Nirvana, which consists in peace.
(Sutrakrtanga: Book 1 Eleventh Lecture: The Path)

I must confess my day-to-day transgressions of the mind, speech and body, through anger, pride, deceit or greed, false behavior and neglect of the Teaching and whatever offence I have committed I here confess, repudiate and repent of it and set aside my past deeds.
(Reverence for the Order: Vandana Formula)

Judaism

One who is slow to wrath is of great understanding.
(Proverbs chapter 14 verse 29)

A soft answer turns away wrath: but grievous words stir up anger.
(Proverbs chapter 15 verse 1)

One who is slow to anger appeases strife.
(Proverbs chapter 15 verse 18)

Hatred stirs up strife: but love covers all sins.
(Proverbs chapter 10 verse 12)

You shall not hate your neighbor in your heart.... You shall not avenge, nor bear any grudge ... but you shall love your neighbor as yourself: I am the Lord.
(Leviticus chapter 19 verses 17–18)

You shall not covet your neighbor's house, you shall not covet your neighbor's wife, nor manservant, nor maidservant, nor ox, nor ass, nor anything that is your neighbor's.
(The Ten Commandments: Commandment No. 10 Exodus chapter 20 verse 17)

I fear not and am not in terror, for it is the Lord my God who goes with me.
(Deuteronomy chapter 31 verse 6)

The Lord is my Light and my Salvation – whom shall I fear or dread? The Lord is the refuge and stronghold of my life – of whom shall I be afraid?
(Psalms chapter 27 verse 1)

You shall not kill.
(The Ten Commandments: Commandment No. 6 Exodus chapter 20 verse 13 and Deuteronomy chapter 5 verse 17)

Judaeo-Christian Apocalyptic Literature
Woe to you who requite your neighbor with evil; for you shall be requited according to your works.
(The Book of Enoch chapter 95 verse 5)

Sikhism

Anger.

(One of five Sikh deadly sins)

Covetousness.

(One of five Sikh deadly sins)

All fear has departed from those who meditate on the fearless God.

(From the Rahiras: Guru Ram Das)

God provides everyone with their daily food; why ... are you afraid? The kulang flies away hundreds of miles, leaving her young behind her. Who feeds them? Who gives them morsels to peck at? Have you not considered this?

(From the Rahiras: Guru Arjan)

Taoism

One should respond to hatred with kindness.

(Lao Tzu, Tao Te Ching (A Consideration of Beginnings) chapter 63)

Identify yourself with non-distinction. Follow the nature of things and admit no personal bias, then the world will be in peace.

(The Domain of Nothingness: Chuang Tzu)

Those who seek immortality must ... extend their humaneness (jen) (compassion) ... even to insects.... Their hands must never injure life.

(The Reward for Deeds: p'ao-p'u Tzu)

Zoroastrianism

Indulge in no wrathfulness, for when one indulges in wrath ... sin and crime of every kind occur unto the mind.
(Commandments for the Body and the Soul)

Avarice and ambition ... will plunge (humanity) into everlasting misery.
(The Vision of Arda-Viraf)

Form no covetous desire, so that the demon of greediness may not deceive thee.... With a greedy person you should not be a partner.
(Commandments for the Body and the Soul)

Be not cruel.... Torment not.
(Admonitions)

Suffer no anxiety, for they who suffer from anxiety become less able to enjoy worldly and spiritual life and contraction happens to the body and soul.
(Commandments for the Body and the Soul)

NDE Accounts

- Anger, greed and negative emotions do not exist in the higher realms.
- There is no fear, blame, judgment, pain or shame in the higher realms; only profound love, peace and unconditional acceptance.
- Struggles, challenges, worries and anxieties are part of the earthly realm; not of the higher realms.
- No hatred, pain or suffering exists in the higher realms.
- Negative energy is incompatible with love and acceptance and therefore does not exist in the higher realms.

- According to universal laws, Earthly existence is based on duality. When negativity no longer exists, one is no longer a resident of this planet as it presently works. Our mission is to acknowledge the existence of this duality and then to prevent negativity from impeding our individual paths by embracing the need for more positivity in our lives. This is the epitome of our life lesson and the beginning of unconditional love and harmony with all life.
- Negative energy held and manifested by humans is a product of their lower level of enlightenment.
- I understood that we must release the density (negative energy) within us that holds back unconditional love and prevents the Light from flowing through us.
- Do not kill or harm other sentient beings as you are also harming yourself. Your life review will surely cause you to empathetically feel personally the harm you have caused to others.
- We harm ourselves when we hurt others. We harm ourselves when we make poor choices which do not serve our highest good and the highest good of all souls around us.
- I was told that there would be no judgment or penalty for having taken my own life. My deed of self-destruction was forgiven. However, the Being of Light told me that I had no right to take my life, or any life for that matter. Only God has authority to give and take a life. Life is sacred and to be cherished. We are all loved unconditionally by the Creator.
- I learned that we must not attempt our self-destruction for to do so is committing the ultimate crime against oneself, against the purpose of this life and against the wisdom of God. God is our Creator but we have been given the power of choice (through Free Will) to shape our own life and final destiny. As soon as I believed in my own worth

and my responsibility to life and to all those around me, my soul was set free.

- Fear does not exist in the Divine realms; it is an instrument of earthly control.
- There is no reason to worry, no reason to fear. Everything happens for a reason and is unfolding as it should.
- Do not fear or grieve for what you have left behind.
- Fear and guilt over things which have gone wrong in our lives are not necessarily justified, as they may be part of our life's learning journey.
- Worry and guilt are negative emotions and energy.
- Worry and fear attract just that into your life.
- Have no fear and no judgment.
- Do not be afraid.
- Have no fear.
- Our negative thoughts and substance abuse can alter human energy. If you emit fear and anger, such emotions will be attracted back to you. Like attracts like.
- Judging others is human folly confined to the earthly realm.
- If we condemn others, we condemn a part of ourselves. Never judge another, but try to understand and empathize.
- To judge others is placing a condition on otherwise Unconditional Love and on life itself.
- One should avoid bias and the temptation to judge others.
- Being judgmental stops the flow of energy and light and produces denser vibrations.
- During my life review I discovered that many trivial events in my past towards which I harbored resentment or held grudges or remembered being injured were actually very different from the way I had remembered them. I had a clear sense that many of these things not only didn't happen in the way that I remembered them

but in fact may well have been due to my shortcomings such as anger, selfishness and greed.

- During a review of my life, I remember seeing my sister at 6 years old and myself at 5. In the review, I was very mean and hateful to my sister, calling her names and making her cry. The Light telepathically informed me of my hatred. At that point, I felt overwhelmed with guilt, shame and humiliation. These feelings were very intense and the worst I have ever known. I had never felt anything with that intensity before and I just wanted the review to end, but it was not over and about to get worse. What I felt next was the worst pain I have ever experienced. Suddenly I realized I had become my sister. I was put inside her so that I could now experience the gut-wrenching pain that she felt due to my actions. I was told by the Light that I had to change my ways by loving instead of hating and that we should love all and hate none.

- Do not feel obliged to lower your vibrations (by drawing upon negative energy) in order to fit in with the ways of the world. To do so will impede your soul's evolutionary progress.

- Do not live your life consumed with self (your own ego and desires) and thereby hurt and let down others.

- Focus on the intent of other people. If their intent is self-focused or negative towards others or disturbs the harmony of Nature and the Universe, it is best to avoid them.

- Each of us has an aura which is the energy field around us. Disease of the body can first be detected in the aura before it manifests in bodily form.

- Illnesses and diseases start on an energetic level before they manifest physically.

Chapter 10

Universal Laws of Karma, Reincarnation and Attraction

Numerous IANDS near death experience accounts include references to, and observations on, so-called universal laws, particularly the Laws of Karma, Reincarnation and Attraction. These universal laws operate both in the higher realms and the Earthly plane of existence but in different contexts and conceptual frameworks.

The Universal Law of Karma essentially postulates, to borrow from a biblical metaphor, that what we sow is what we ultimately reap. All that we send forth into the Universe is sooner or later returned to us. A wise or compassionate act will produce good results; an ignorant or careless act will produce negative results and harmful consequences. It is a universal or natural law of cause and effect and of action and reaction. Every volitional act produces effects or results. The effects and consequences of our acts ripple outwards to eternity. It is not really a system of reward or punishment or retributive justice but operates in virtue of its own nature as a universal law. In other words, it is what it is. Karma is the sum of a person's actions in this and previous states of existence which determine their fate in future existences. What happens in a previous life directly impacts the *atma* or soul in the next life, either positively or negatively. Karma is a concept from Hinduism, Buddhism and Sikhism which has some biblical parallels as we shall see below.

According to religious and philosophical beliefs concerning reincarnation, the soul or spirit, after physical death of the body, begins a new life in a new body that may be human or animal depending on the moral quality of actions from the previous lifetime. It is a belief held by many mainstream Eastern religions and belief systems. However, the unanimous view or conviction of those who have undergone a near death experience is that reincarnation transcends belief and is a certain fact or Universal Law. Perfection cannot be attained in a single lifetime. Reincarnation is the evolution of consciousness – it gives us the opportunity to gradually evolve spiritually through various valuable learning experiences we acquire in our different incarnations. The soul carries with it the essence of an incarnation's experience into a new birth. When our soul-consciousness becomes totally liberated and is subsumed in the Light, we lack nothing and thereby transcend desire. The cycle of repeated births and deaths is broken.

The essence of the Universal Law of Attraction is that like understands and attracts like and that it manifests or creates the things we are thinking of. The Roman Emperor Marcus Aurelius once observed that our life is what our thoughts make it (from *Meditations*). We create or manifest not only with our acts but with our thoughts and words. What we think and speak about and the manner in which it is done draws similar energy to us. Positive thoughts and words attract positive energy unto you; negative thoughts and words attract negative energy unto you. We become what we think and speak of. We create for ourselves what we focus on. What we think and speak about, we bring about. In other words, our thoughts and words create our own reality or experience (as well as our delusions and projections). We must take care in what we think and say as thoughts and words create our Earthly reality and can harm others. Our thoughts shape the essence of who and what we are, so we must guard our thoughts carefully. What our soul's energy emits draws similar energy back to us, for good or for bad. Therefore, long for and focus on God/Source and the Higher Realms and your soul will be drawn there. The Universal Law of Attraction teaches that through focus of the mind, one is able to create their own reality in all aspects of life by asking, believing and receiving. Attracting what we need into our life requires us to believe we will receive it and acting with certainty that we can and will receive it. We must be grateful for what we have requested but not yet received as if we have already received it. The virtual premise underlying the Law of Attraction is succinctly expressed in the New Testament verse from the Book of Mark: "What things soever you desire, when you pray, believe that you receive them, and you shall have them" (Mark chapter 11 verse 24).

The Universal Law of Karma

Scriptural References
Buddhism

All that we are is the result of what we have thought.... If one speaks or acts with a pure mind, happiness follows them as one's shadow.
(The Dhammapada chapter 1 (The Twin-Verses) verse 2)

If one speaks or acts with an evil thought, pain follows them, as the wheel follows the foot of the ox that draws the carriage.
(The Dhammapada chapter 1 (The Twin-Verses) verse 1)

Whosoever offends an innocent person, pure and guiltless, their evil comes back upon them like fine dust thrown against the wind.
(The Dhammapada chapter 9 (Evil) verse 125)

Christianity

All who draw the sword will die by the sword.
(Matthew chapter 26 verse 52)

Those who sow sparingly shall reap also sparingly; and those who sow bountifully shall reap also bountifully.
(2 Corinthians chapter 9 verse 6)

Whatsoever one sows, that shall they reap.
(Galatians chapter 6 verse 7)

Peacemakers who sow in peace reap a harvest of righteousness.
(James chapter 3 verse 18)

Hinduism

According as one acts, according as one conducts themselves, so do they become. The doer of good becomes good. The doer of evil becomes evil. One becomes virtuous by virtuous action, bad by bad action.
(Brhadaranyaka Upanisad)

As is one's desire, such is one's resolve; as is one's resolve, such the action one performs; what action (*karma*) one performs, that one procures for themselves.
(Brhadaranyaka Upanisad)

According unto their deeds, the embodied one successively assumes forms in various conditions. Coarse and fine, many in number, the embodied one chooses forms according to their own qualities (the soul's *karma* determines the subsequent incarnation).
(Svetasvatara Upanisad)

Even as a calf finds its mother among a thousand cows, an act formerly done is sure to find the perpetrator.
(Vaisnava-dharma-sastra 20: 31–53)

Jainism

A rare chance, in the long course of time, is human birth for a living being.... Thus the soul which suffers for its carelessness is driven about in the round of rebirth by its good and bad *karma*.
(The Simile of the Leaf: Uttaradhyayana)

Judaism

Those who plow evil and those who sow trouble reap it.
(Job chapter 4 verse 8)

Whoever seeks good finds favor, but mischief comes to one who searches for it.
(Proverbs chapter 11 verse 27)

Whoever digs a pit will fall into it; if someone rolls a stone, it will roll back on them.
(Proverbs chapter 26 verse 27)

The trouble they cause recoils on them; their violence comes down on their heads.
(Psalms chapter 7 verse 16)

Sikhism

The body is the field of *karma* and in this age, whatever you shall plant, you shall harvest.
(Guru Granth Sahib 78)

Zen Buddhism

Life is an echo. What you send out, comes back. What you sow, you reap. What you give, you get. What you see in others, exists in you. Remember, life is an echo. It always gets back to you. So give goodness.
(Zen proverb)

NDE Accounts

- All that we send out comes back to us.
- What we put out in the Universe returns to us.
- What you create is yours.
- As you sow, you reap. Sow love and it shall be returned manifold although you do not intend or expect it. The more we sow on Earth, the more we will reap in Heaven.
- My near death experience taught me that we reap what we sow and that no purpose in life is too small or insignificant in God's eyes.
- There are *karmic* reasons for both the good and the bad in our lives.
- Souls are reincarnated. The soul's past lives and fears and unresolved problems accumulated therein may be affecting its current Earthly existence.
- The quality of person that you are in this life directly affects your quality of life in the next phase of your evolutionary journey.
- What lies ahead for us depends on how we have lived and learned from our current existence.
- Cause and effect do exist in the higher realms but outside of our Earthly conception of them.
- The things we do on Earth do matter. The consequences and effects of words, acts and non-action ripple through an eternity.

The Universal Law of Reincarnation

Scriptural References
Buddhism

This is my last birth. There is no more becoming for me.
(The First Sermon: Vinaya, Mahavagga)

It is craving that leads back to birth ... the craving for sensual pleasure, the craving to be born again.
(The First Sermon: Vinaya, Mahavagga)

Virtuous and endowed with insight, one gives up attachment to sense-desires. Verily one does not return to enter a womb again (is not reincarnated).
(Sutta Nipata: 1 Uragavagga 8 Mettasutta 10 verse 151)

When you go to the other shore of existence, if your mind is altogether free, you will not again enter into birth and decay.
(The Dhammapada chapter 24 (Thirst) verse 348)

Hinduism
Death is certain for one who has been born, and rebirth is inevitable for one who has died.
(Bhagavad-Gita chapter 2 verse 27)

The embodied one successively assumes forms in various conditions. Coarse and fine, many in number, the embodied one chooses forms according to their own qualities.
(Svetasvatara Upanisad)

As a goldsmith, taking a piece of gold, reduces it to another newer and more beautiful form, just so this soul, striking down this body and dispelling its ignorance, makes for itself another newer and more beautiful form.
(Brhadaranyaka Upanisad)

Jainism
The soul which suffers for its carelessness is driven about in the round of rebirth by its good and bad *karma*.
(The Simile of the Leaf: Uttaradhyayana)

If a monk is attached to vanities and desires fame, they will suffer again and again in the Circle of Births.
(Sutrakrtanga: Book 1 Thirteenth Lecture: The Real Truth)

In this world the causes of sin must be comprehended and renounced. Those who do not comprehend and renounce the causes of sin are born again and again in manifold births and experience all painful feelings.
(Acaranga Sutra: Book 1 First Lecture First Lesson: Knowledge of the Weapon)

Those who indulge themselves in worldly pleasures are born again and again.
(Acaranga Sutra: Book 1 Fourth Lecture First Lesson: Righteousness)

Sikhism
They whom God awakens and causes to drink the essence of His word, know the story of the Ineffable Embrace for which you have come into the world and God ... will dwell in your heart. You shall find a home with comfort and peace in God's own palace and not return again in this world.
(From the Sohila: Guru Arjan)

NDE Accounts
- Outside of my body, I learned that reincarnation of the soul is a universal law.
- We have had many past lives. Only the body dies; the spirit/soul was made for an eternity. We have all passed through many lives. Our soul-energy cannot be destroyed.
- My out-of-body experience imparted to me that I have lived on Earth many times before.

- As a result of my near death experience, I now believe in reincarnation.
- I was shown in great detail the choice of reincarnation.
- My belief in reincarnation and *karma* has been strengthened by my out-of-body experience. I now have certain knowledge and proof thereof.
- Death of the physical body is a prelude to the soul-consciousness undergoing a life review to reflect on what it learned from that lifetime to prepare for its next incarnation.
- The quality of person that you are in this life directly affects your quality of life in the next phase of your evolutionary journey.
- We keep coming back until we have learned all of the lessons and get it right.
- Souls are reincarnated and can be either sex in previous lifetimes.
- Souls are reincarnated. The soul's past lives and fears and unresolved problems accumulated therein may be affecting its current Earthly existence.
- Learning continues throughout eternity. The soul's destiny is to seek to acquire universal knowledge both in its Earthly incarnations and in the afterlife.
- Life in the earthly realm is a soul journey and venturing forth to learn; physical death is a returning home for the soul's rest and debriefing before its next incarnation.
- After every life we live we become stronger and truer, tempered by our experiences until such time as we may complete our journey and we are truly born.
- Each Earthly lifetime is a chapter in a book detailing our soul's evolutionary journey. During the living of each lifetime, we sometimes forget who we truly are but the

recollection returns when we depart our physical body and return Home to Heaven.

- The journey of our soul is an eternal learning and evolutionary process, interspersed between countless spiritual realms and physical incarnations.

The Universal Law of Attraction

Scriptural References
Buddhism

All that we are is the result of what we have thought: it is founded on our thoughts, it is made up of our thoughts.
(The Dhammapada chapter 1 (The Twin-Verses) verse 2)

To dwell on the highest thoughts, this is the teaching of the Awakened.
(The Dhammapada chapter 14 (The Buddha/The Awakened) verse 185)

Let your thoughts of boundless love pervade the whole world.
(Sutta Nipata: Uragavagga, Mettasutta chapter 1.8.8 verse 149)

Christianity

What things soever you desire, when you pray, believe that you receive them, and you shall have them.
(Mark chapter 11 verse 24)

Ask, and it shall be given you…. For every one that asks receives.
(Matthew chapter 7 verses 7–8)

And all things, whatsoever you shall ask in prayer, believing, you shall receive.
(Matthew chapter 21 verse 22)

Those who live by the sword shall die by the sword.
(Matthew chapter 26 verse 52)

Set your thoughts on things above, not on things on the earth.
(Colossians chapter 3 verse 2)

In every thing by prayer and supplication with thanksgiving let
your requests be made known unto God.
(Philippians chapter 4 verse 6)

Hinduism

All that one gives to others one gives to one's self.
(The Teachings of Bhagavan Sri Ramana Maharshi: Who Am I?
(Nan Yar?))

Jainism

Have equanimity (calmness and mental poise) towards all.
(The Lay Person's Inner Voyage: Nityanaimittika-pathavali)

Judaism

For as one thinks in their heart, so are they (our thoughts reflect
where our heart is and who we are becoming).
(Proverbs chapter 23 verse 7)

Zoroastrianism

I praise the well-thought, well-spoken, well-performed thoughts,
words and works (deeds).... I abandon all evil thoughts, words
and works.
(The Creed)

NDE Accounts

- Everything we experience in life we are attracting into it. We become what we think about most. Our thoughts manifest or become things and have their own frequency and energy.
- We become what we think about.
- Our thoughts are our essence.
- Your thoughts and your feelings create your life and your own reality.
- You attract to yourself whatever the thoughts you have inside you.
- What we think about, we bring about. What we focus on, we will get.
- Like attracts like. Positive attracts positive; negative attracts negative.
- If you are negative and suffering, others absorb it; if you are loving and positive, others absorb it.
- Worry and fear attract just that into your life.
- If you emit fear and anger, such emotions will be attracted back to you.
- Focus on what you want rather than on what you do not want. What our mind focuses upon, we will receive.
- Cleanse your thought process. Thoughts are very powerful; and as you think, so you are. They have creative effects in this world and in the Universe.
- Open yourself up to the abundance of the Universe and you will attract it into your life.
- Like understands like. To understand and relate to any of the higher realms or dimensions, you must open up your soul to that particular realm or dimension.

Chapter 11

The Golden Rule: The Essential Message for Humanity

"Do unto others as you would have them do unto you" (New Testament: Luke chapter 6 verse 31). In other words, never do to, or impose on, others what you would not desire or be prepared to do for yourself. Treat others as you would wish to be treated.

This concise maxim represents a principle of conduct which has a potentially profound impact on our relations with others and represents a fundamental tenet of many faiths and belief systems. There are few other ethical exhortations which so forcefully and succinctly capture the essence of how we should interact with others.

From a Confucian perspective, the principle of reciprocity or mutuality constitutes the essence of propriety (the conventional standard of proper behavior) or proper conduct in society, while from a Western perspective, the Golden Rule postulates a mutual exchange of respect, care, toleration and deference (respectful or courteous regard). From a Buddhist perspective, the principle is essentially non-dualistic in eliminating the distinction between self and others (or, to put it another way, emphasizing the connectivity or oneness between us all). For, as some of those who have undergone a near death experience report (see below), what we do to another, we do to ourself. Some faiths, such as Buddhism and Jainism, extend the operation of the Golden Rule to encompass the treatment of all sentient or living beings by humanity.

Although not frequently mentioned by those who have undergone a near death experience, the so-called Golden Rule is mentioned from time to time in their accounts and observations, some of which follow below.

Scriptural References
Buddhism

All tremble at punishment, all fear death; remember you are like unto them, so do not kill, nor cause slaughter (as life is dear to oneself, it is dear also to other living beings: by comparing oneself with others, we bestow pity on all beings).
(The Dhammapada chapter 10 (Punishment) verse 129)

Christianity

Do to others what you would have them do to you, for this sums up the Law and the Prophets.
(Matthew chapter 7 verse 12)

Do unto others as you would have them do unto you.
(Luke chapter 6 verse 31)

Honor (respect) all you encounter.
(1 Peter chapter 2 verse 17)

Confucianism

The feeling of respect is the beginning of propriety.
(The Innateness of the Four Great Virtues: Mencius)

Tzu-kung asked: Is there one word which can express the essence of right conduct in life? Confucius replied: "It is the word *shu* – reciprocity: Do not do to others what you do not want them to do to you."
(Analects)

Jainism

This is the quintessence of wisdom: not to kill anything. Know this to be the legitimate conclusion from the principle of the reciprocity with regard to non-killing.

(Sutrakrtanga: Book 1 Eleventh Lecture: The Path)

Indifferent to worldly objects, humanity should wander about treating all creatures (sentient beings) in the world as they themselves would wish to be treated.

(Sutrakrtanga: Book 1 Eleventh Lecture: The Path)

Judaism

You shall not ... bear any grudge against (others), but you shall love your neighbor as yourself.

(Leviticus chapter 19 verse 18)

Taoism

Those who seek immortality must ... treat others as they treat themselves.

(The Reward for Deeds: p'ao-p'u Tzu)

NDE Accounts

- All religions are merely vain attempts to express a simple Truth. The Golden Rule (do unto others as you would have them do unto you) is the central rule to live our lives by.
- I was told by the Light to connect with others in a positive way, to look for the good in them and to live by the "golden rule."
- Treat yourself the way you would want others to treat you. If you love and respect yourself, you will love others.
- We are all one in the Universe. When we harm others, we harm our own soul.
- What is done to one is done to all. We are all one. Therefore to hurt someone else is to hurt oneself.

Chapter 12

The Immortal Soul-Consciousness

For millennia, philosophers, theologians and metaphysicists have pondered the question of what it means to be human and exactly what we are comprised of. Are we more than our physical bodies? When our body dies, does our awareness end in an empty void of nothingness or does part of us continue in the form of what has been variously described as a soul, spirit, life-force or consciousness? And what is the relationship between such consciousness and the functioning human brain? Does consciousness depend exclusively thereon or is it transcendental in nature, existing outside of a functioning brain, existing prior to and after a human incarnation or embodiment?

The scriptural references cited below all conclude that each of us has a soul which has been bequeathed to us by God and to whom our soul returns. The soul is eternal and cannot be destroyed. Some of those who have undergone a near death experience report some remarkable and definitive observations on these issues and questions which go far beyond what may be found or discerned in religious scripture. They observe consistently that our consciousness survives the death of our physical body and indeed does not depend on a functioning human brain. Our consciousness survives the death of our body and brain. The brain merely serves as a conduit or filter respectively enabling and limiting access to universal knowledge, awareness and connection to the higher realms. Consciousness is described as transcendental, limitless and eternal energy. Consciousness is our true essence, our mind, sense-perception, thoughts, feelings and emotions and who and what we truly are at the deepest and most basic level of existence. It transcends all physical/material matter and is a foundational building-block of all that is and of the Ultimate Reality (see above Chapter 6). Outside of our physical body, our soul is a receptor to elevated awareness and expanded consciousness. Our physical bodies are mere temporary homes enabling us to pursue our Earthly mission.

What follows is a cross-section of scriptural references to the soul and the most noteworthy written IANDS account observations that speak to these issues and offer revelations on the true nature of that aspect of the human being which I shall refer to as the soul-consciousness.

Scriptural References
Baha'i
Empty yourselves of doubts ... that you may be prepared for Eternal Life and ready to meet God. Herein there is no death.
(Of The Light: Words of Wisdom from the Supreme Pen of Baha'u'llah)

Beyond this material (physical) body, man is endowed with another reality.... This other and inner reality is called the heavenly body.
('Abdu'l-Baha)

Buddhism
The mind takes possession of everything not only on Earth, but also in Heaven, and immortality is the securest treasure-trove.
(The Buddha)

Consciousness – *vijnana* – is invisible, boundless, all-penetrating, and the basis of body, sensation, perception and will.
(The Buddha, Dighna Nikaya, IV)

Christianity

Fear not they who kill the body, but are not able to kill the soul.
(Matthew chapter 10 verse 28)

For what is one profited, if they shall gain the whole world, and lose their own soul?
(Matthew chapter 16 verse 26)

You shall love the Lord your God with all your heart, and with all your soul, and with all your mind.
(Matthew chapter 22 verse 37)

There are celestial (heavenly) bodies and terrestrial (earthly) bodies.
(1 Corinthians chapter 15 verse 40)

Look not at the things which are seen (the physical world), but at the things which are not seen (the spiritual realm): for the things which are seen are temporal; but the things which are not seen are eternal.
(2 Corinthians chapter 4 verse 18)

Hinduism

The Self (soul) is eternal and immutable (cannot be altered or destroyed). When the body dies, the Self does not die.
(Katha Upanisad)

The soul (*atman*) is infinite, universal.... What is perishable is Primary Matter (the body). What is immortal and imperishable is *Hara* (the soul).
(Svetasvatara Upanisad)

The *atman* (individual soul/self) can give no reason for grief, for they are immortal. One does not mourn over the embodied *atman* when it passes from one stage (incarnation) to another ... the nature of the (physical) body is perishable and serves to enable the innate *atman* to undergo accumulated *karma* ... nobody can kill the *atman* which is not born when the body is born and does not die when the body dies.... The innate *atman* cannot be destroyed, even if its (physical) body be destroyed.... The *atman* is essentially eternal.
(Ramanuja on the Atman and Body: Commentary to the Bhagavad-Gita)

No weapons will hurt the (soul), no fire burn it, no waters moisten it, and no wind dry it up ... it is imperishable, perpetual, unchanging, immovable, without beginning.
(Vaisnava-dharma-sastra chapter 20 verses 39–53)

O seeker, know the true nature of your soul.... O Lord, (may we attain) the everlasting consciousness of Supreme Light and Joy.
(Yajur Veda)

The nature of Awareness is existence-consciousness-bliss.... What is called "mind" is a wondrous power residing in the Self. It causes all thoughts to arise. Apart from thoughts, there is no such thing as mind. Therefore, thought is the nature of mind.... It is the mind that is called the subtle body or the soul.
(The Teachings of Bhagavan Sri Ramana Maharshi: Who Am I? (Nan Yar?))

Islam

People, be mindful of your Lord, who created you from a single soul.
(The Women chapter 4 verse 1)

I have breathed My Spirit into (Adam, the first man).
(Al-Hijr chapter 15 verse 29)

Jainism

One and eternal is my soul, characterized by intuition, insight
and knowledge.
(The Lay Person's Inner Voyage: Nityanaimittika-pathavali)

Judaism

The Lord God formed man of the dust of the ground, and
breathed into his nostrils the breath of life; and man became a
living soul.
(Genesis chapter 2 verse 7)

You shall love the Lord your God with all your heart, and with
all your soul, and with all your might.
(Deuteronomy chapter 6 verse 5)

Thus saith God the Lord, he that created the heavens, and
stretched them out; he that spread forth the earth, and that
which comes out of it; he that gives breath unto the people upon
it, and spirit to them that walk therein.
(Isaiah chapter 42 verse 5)

(The Lord) restoreth my soul.
(Psalms chapter 23 verse 3)

Then shall the dust return to the earth as it was: and the spirit
shall return unto God who gave it.
(Ecclesiastes chapter 12 verse 7)

Behold, all souls are mine (the Lord God's).
(Ezekiel chapter 18 verse 4)

Sikhism

By His (God's) order bodies are produced.... By His order souls are infused into them.

(Guru Nanak's Japji)

Zoroastrianism

Recollect that your body will return to dust, but your soul, if rich in good works, will mount to immortality.... Take less care of your body and more of your soul.

(The Vision of Arda-Viraf)

You should not become presumptuous through life; for death comes upon you at last and the perishable part falls to the ground.

(Commandments for the Body and the Soul)

NDE Accounts

- The soul is conscious-energy.
- We are much more than flesh, bones and blood.
- You are more than your physical body; you are your spirit and this is the true reality.
- Our soul comprises the core essence within us that truly makes us who and what we are.
- Although you can access consciousness with your brain, it exists outside the body. It is not contained in the brain. It is eternal and exists without a physical body.
- Our life does not begin and end on Earth.
- There is life after death, but this entails loss of your Earthly personal identity.
- After my near death experience, life is so much more precious to me. I believe that everything has spirit-consciousness.

- The events in our lives pass and are no more and will never happen again, but God and our souls are eternal.
- We are immortal because we have souls that never die.
- Our soul is energy, light, essence and consciousness. Our soul is infinite and eternal, transcending space and time.
- Humans are an eternal soul in a physical body or shell experiencing life in a material realm known as Earth.
- Our consciousness is our soul which goes on forever and expands in the higher realms or dimensions. It is our eternal essence and is only housed temporarily in our bodies.
- Outside the body, consciousness and knowing awareness are vastly expanded.
- The soul's temporary home is the physical body. The soul is the incorporeal and conscious aspect of human existence.
- The soul exists in a disembodied state in the higher realms.
- Our souls are light, frequency, vibrations and love.
- My near death experience was a wonderful gift. I now know that consciousness exists beyond the physical body and that death is but a door we pass through.
- In truth, we really never sleep; only our bodies do. We are always aware and active on one level of consciousness or another. The fact that we dream while asleep is an indication of our consciousness always being active. Our bodies need to rest so that we can tap into and experience other aspects of our consciousness and being. The best way I can describe the transition from being "alive" on the physical Earthly plane and the passage to the Other Side is the passage from one room to another. You do not cease to be or lose consciousness; your consciousness simply shifts from one vantage point to another. Your outlook

and feelings change. The feelings were profound and became that peace which surpasses all understanding.

- As a result of my near death experience, I no longer just believe but I know beyond doubt that we are so much more than our physical bodies. We are part of a larger body of consciousness. We can hardly even begin to comprehend and appreciate the beauty and complexity of our true nature as incredibly powerful spiritual beings.
- Our consciousness is pure thought.
- Pure consciousness is energy glowing with intelligence and love.
- It is the essence, rather than the manifestation, of a person or thing which really matters and is the reality.
- Remember who you truly are.
- Penetrate the depths of your consciousness to unlock the eternal Truths.
- Every soul is special but no better or worse than others. The Light loves us all but we each have different paths.

Chapter 13

Liberation of the Soul-Consciousness

Albert Einstein once said that the true value of a human being is determined by the measure and sense in which they have obtained liberation from the self. What does this mean and how may it be attained? According to Simone Weil, attachment is the greatest fabricator of illusions; the ultimate reality can be attained only by someone who is detached. We must therefore free ourselves as much as we can from the illusions and distractions of this Earthly plane. Although we must be in this world to evolve and elevate our soul-consciousness, it is not necessary to be of this world.

How can we detach from this world? Spiritual and religious teachings and sages and seers have pondered this very question for millennia. Detachment is the antithesis of a desire to acquire, accumulate and to get one's way all the time. It is a detachment from things and objects which are transitory and impermanent by nature. Detachment is separation from this world and all of its distractions and illusions. It is a letting go; an understanding of the relative unimportance and transient nature of personal power, fame and wealth. It is a renunciation of the ways of the world, worldly riches and material objects; a letting go of grasping, clinging and distraction (including negative feelings). It is an overcoming of obsession and compulsion for worldly pleasures, prestige and affluence sought by many. Detachment is a cessation of desire and craving, a suppression of one's covetous nature, ego and sensual appetites, and a loss of interest in worldly amusements, pleasures and self-preoccupation and self-identification. Detachment is a letting go of things which must be parted with in any event on the death of the physical body. We enter this world with nothing and depart therefrom with nothing, apart from the treasures of, and love within, the heart and soul accumulated over an incarnated lifetime. In short, it is living a simple and uncomplicated life in the spirit rather than in the world. Liberation of the soul-consciousness from these attachments produces peace, contentment and an elevation and expansion of consciousness or spiritual awakening. According to the Hindu *Mandukya Upanisad*, the fourth stage of consciousness (*turiya*) is that of transcendental consciousness in which the duality between the observer and the observed becomes one. The soul-consciousness becomes truly egoless and is absorbed into the Light or *Om*.

Proceeding deeper within the higher spiritual realms entails a realignment of thought as to what really matters and what is real as opposed to illusory – an engagement in a process of "unlearning" and "relearning" as it were. It is like seeing for the first time; an opening of the mind to the limitless potential and possibilities that an infinite and abundant Universe has to offer. Numerous accounts of those who have undergone a near death experience point to various fallacious human or Earthly constructs which have been deconstructed for them by their learnings in the higher spiritual realms. These include, among others, our human misunderstanding of the concept or notion of "death" associated with the demise of the physical body (to be discussed in more detail in the next chapter) and the constraining and sometimes debilitating nature of social, cultural and belief systems on our ability to perceive eternal Truths and Universal Laws. Fear is yet another illusion to be cast off. Some fear living while others fear dying. This fear may be so consuming that we fail to live our lives to the full and remain oblivious to the purpose of, and meaning to, our life. And those who fear change in their lives should accept it as a natural consequence of the operation of the Laws of the

Universe. We must seek to free ourselves from these illusions in order to recall the true nature of our soul-consciousness and what our Earthly purpose is. This is the path to self-realization and enlightenment.

Scriptural References
Baha'i

All human beings are earthly; the hearts are connected with this world. Day and night their thoughts and occupations are earthly; all belong to the world. They think about the honors of this world or about the riches and wealth of this world or of name or fame in this world.... If you see one whose heart is attached to this world and in whom there is no ... detachment or turning to God ... then you will know that they are a tree of darkness.
(True Belief: Words of Wisdom from the Supreme Pen of Baha'u'llah)

If you love Me, turn away from yourself; if my Will you seek, regard not your own; that you may die in Me and I live in you.
(Of Divine Humanity: Words of Wisdom from the Supreme Pen of Baha'u'llah)

Buddhism

One is the road that leads to (worldly) wealth, another road that leads to Nirvana; knowing this fact, the disciples of Buddha will not yearn for honor (glory), but will strive for separation from the world.
(The Dhammapada chapter 5 (The Fool) verse 75)

Detachment (the suppression of desires and cravings) is the best of states.
(The Dhammapada chapter 19 (The Just) verse 272)

With the relinquishing of all thought and egotism, the enlightened one is liberated through not clinging.
(Majjhima Nikaya chapter 72 verse 15)

Christianity

Blessed are the poor in spirit (humble and simple and detached from worldly ways): for theirs is the Kingdom of Heaven.
(Matthew chapter 5 verse 3)

Do not store up for yourselves treasures on earth (material or worldly wealth) ... but store up for yourselves treasures in heaven (spiritual treasures of the heart).
(Matthew chapter 6 verses 19–20)

We bring nothing (material or physical) into the world, and we cannot take anything out of the world.
(1 Timothy chapter 6 verses 6–7)

Keep yourself unspoiled by the world (and its ways).
(James chapter 1 verse 27)

Hinduism

Renunciation (Detachment).
(Saintly Virtue No. 13 of those endowed with a Divine Nature: Bhagavad-Gita chapter 16 verses 1–3)

Wholly trained in renunciation, released, you will come to God.
(Everything is a Sacrifice to Me: Bhagavad-Gita chapter 9)

When the world which is what-is-seen has been removed (perceived as unreal or illusory), there will be self-realization ... self-realization will not be gained unless the belief that the world is real is removed.... When the mind, which is the cause of all

cognitions and of all actions, becomes quiescent, the world will disappear.... As thoughts arise, destroying them utterly without any residue in the very place of their origin is non-attachment.... The thought "who am I?" will destroy all other thoughts, and like the stick used for stirring the burning pyre, it will itself in the end get destroyed. Then, there will arise self-realization.
(The Teachings of Bhagavan Sri Ramana Maharshi: Who Am I? (Nan Yar?))

When the mind stays in the heart, the "I" which is the source of all thoughts will go, and the Self (soul-consciousness) which ever exists will shine. Whatever one does, one should do without the egoity "I." If one acts in that way, all will appear as of the nature of Siva (God) ... the mind of the one who knows the Truth does not leave Brahman. The mind of the ignorant, on the contrary, revolves in the world, feeling miserable ... what is called the world is only thought. When the world disappears, i.e. when there is no thought, the mind experiences happiness; and when the world appears, it goes through misery.
(The Teachings of Bhagavan Sri Ramana Maharshi: Who Am I? (Nan Yar?))

There will come a time when one will have to forget all that one has learned.
(The Teachings of Bhagavan Sri Ramana Maharshi: Who Am I? (Nan Yar?))

There is no happiness in any object of the world. We imagine through our ignorance that we derive happiness from objects.... The mind should not be allowed to wander towards worldly objects ... desire ... should be eschewed.... Desireless is refraining from turning the mind towards any object.
(The Teachings of Bhagavan Sri Maharshi: Who Am I? (Nan Yar?))

The highest Self, all endless bliss, the unconditioned limitless consciousness, being realized ... let one lose themselves in the ecstasy of Realization, for they have lost all touch with bondage of every description.
(Svarajyasiddhi)

Islam

The life of this world as compared with the Hereafter is but a brief passing enjoyment.
(The Thunder chapter 13 verse 26)

The life of this world is only an illusory pleasure.
(Iron chapter 57 verse 20)

People love the transient life of this world but neglect the Hereafter.
(The Resurrection chapter 75 verses 20–1)

Jainism

Subdue your Self (ego), for the Self is difficult to subdue; if your Self is subdued, you will be happy in this world and in the next.
(Uttaradhyayana: First Lecture: On Discipline)

Liberation is attained by conquering the will.
Uttaradhyayana: Fourth Lecture: Impurity)

The wise ... knowing the nature of excessive pride and deceit, giving them all up, bring about their liberation.
(Sutrakrtanga: Book 1 Eleventh Lecture: The Path)

I renounce all attachments, whether ... small or great.
(Fifth Great Vow: Acaranga Sutra)

Cast aside from you all attachments, as the lotus lets drop the pure monsoon water.
(The Simile of the Leaf: Uttaradhyayana)

A wise person should abstain from seeking fame, glory and renown ... (and) all pleasures in the whole world.
(Sutrakrtanga: Book 1 Ninth Lecture: The Law)

Judaism
Those who make themselves poor (by practicing austerities and detachment) have great riches (spiritual treasures of the heart).
(Proverbs chapter 13 verse 7)

Those who love (worldly) pleasure shall be poor (lacking in spiritual awareness and treasures).
(Proverbs chapter 21 verse 17)

To search your own glory is not glory.
(Proverbs chapter 25 verse 27)

Judaeo-Christian Apocalyptic Literature
Woe to you, ye rich, for you have trusted in your riches, and from your riches shall you (eventually) depart, because you have not remembered (been mindful of) the Most High in the days of your riches.
(The Book of Enoch chapter 94 verse 8)

Perfect Liberty Kyodan (modernized Shinto)
Our true self is revealed when our ego is effaced.
(Twenty-One Precepts No. 6)

Sikhism

O God, let our minds be for ever humble. O God, save us from the sin of egoism.
(The Community and its Past Saints: A Congregational Prayer)

Those whose hearts are full of love ... are in bliss because they have no love of self. Only those who love God conquer love of self.
(Spiritual Marriage: The Bara Mah)

O God, save us from the sin of attachment.
(The Community and its Past Saints: A Congregational Prayer)

Taoism

Lessen the self (pride/ego).
(Lao Tzu, Tao Te Ching (Return to Simplicity) chapter 19)

They who practice Tao daily diminish. Again and again they humble themselves.
(Lao Tzu, Tao Te Ching (To Forget Knowledge) chapter 48)

To recognize one's insignificance (in the vast scheme of things) is called enlightenment.... This is called practicing the eternal.
(Lao Tzu, Tao Te Ching (Return to Origin) chapter 52)

The wise learn to be unlearned; they return to that which all others ignore.
(Lao Tzu, Tao Te Ching (Consider the Insignificant) chapter 64)

They who are eternally without worldly desire perceive the spiritual side.
(Lao Tzu, Tao Te Ching (What is the Tao) chapter 1)

Ignoring the things which awaken desire keeps the heart undisturbed.
(Lao Tzu, Tao Te Ching (Quieting People) chapter 3)

Diminish desire.
(Lao Tzu, Tao Te Ching (Return to Simplicity) chapter 19)

Zen Buddhism

To forget the self (overcome the ego) is to be awakened by all things.
(Dogen)

We accept the graceful falling of mountain cherry blossoms. But it is much harder for us to fall away from our attachments to the world.
(Zen Wisdom)

Relearn everything. Let every moment be a new beginning.
(Zen proverb)

Zoroastrianism

You should not become presumptuous through much treasure and wealth; for in the end it is necessary for you to leave all.
(Commandments for the Body and the Soul)

NDE Accounts

- Relinquish your thoughts and ego and merge with the Light.
- There is no "I." It is an illusion of the physical (earthly) realm.
- In the spiritual realms, there is no sense of time or self.
- Do not live your life consumed with self (your own ego) and thereby hurt and let down others.

- Relinquish your ego and enjoy expansive and liberated consciousness.
- Extinguish your ego.
- Self-realization or enlightenment is the extinguishment of self and separation.
- Your mind is limitless. Do not be deluded by your finite physical body. We are unlimited spiritual beings.
- I learned during my life review that power, wealth and fame mean nothing in the higher realms.
- What my life review taught me was that the most extraordinary and significant moments of our lives are not what we consider them to be – wealth, possessions, fame, promotions etc. What we consider to be ... small kindnesses ... are the most significant.
- The free (liberated) soul cares not for identity (ego) or wealth or fame. It does not carry the burden of worry or anxiety. It does not fear life on Earth or departure therefrom. This is what God calls us to become and why we are here on Earth.
- Earthly matters we associate with our self or ego dissipate and are meaningless in the higher realms.
- When your soul leaves your body, you become detached from the earthly realm and become an emotionally neutral and distant observer of events therein.
- What we consider important in the earthly realm is insignificant and superficial (intranscendental) in the higher spiritual realms.
- In order to spiritually evolve and graduate into the higher spiritual realms, we must learn to let go of our attachments to the current realm of existence we inhabit. These hold us back.
- Our souls cannot be truly liberated and enlightened and perceive the Universe wholly and accurately until they

are liberated from the distractions and attachments of the world and all its illusions.

- Do not fill the empty void within you with the things of this world.
- Unclutter your mind. Detach from the material world.
- It is not about what you materially possess, but what you have given to others.
- One needs to ponder what things are preventing us from living our earthly life to the fullest. We need to change ourselves accordingly.
- One's belief systems may be perceived in the spiritual realms to be severely limiting and constraining.
- Do not fear death and the unknown; upon re-birth in the spirit world, all-knowingness returns.
- Do not fear the unknown because your soul has always known that there is nothing which is unknowable.
- Do not fret over petty things.
- Do not fear living or dying.
- Do not fear death as it is illusory.
- Accept your own mortality and embrace your eventual (physical) death. Release your fear of death and live a fuller life and feel more alive.
- "Dying" is a human-created Earth term or construct that means little in the spiritual realms.
- Fear of death is human error. Our souls are eternal.
- Fear of death prevents many from living their life to the full and achieving their soul's mission.
- I no longer fear death as I know now from my (out-of-body) experience that my soul survives my bodily death.
- There is no need to fear physical death as your consciousness survives it. Your death in the physical realm re-births you into the spiritual realm.

- People fear death, like a thief in the night no one can avoid. I know this to be farthest from the truth. Within death, there is a complete cleansing of the spirit, a washing away of our realities of the flesh and an awakening of the spirit to truths no language can begin to describe. Death is a beginning, not a destination.
- When you have gone beyond the veil and returned to your body, you will no longer fear death; in fact, you will long for it.
- Do not feel obliged to lower your vibrations in order to fit in with the ways of the world. To do so will impede your soul's evolutionary progress.
- Everything in our life is fluid. Nothing remains the same. Every living thing grows and changes. Do not fear change. Let go of your security blanket as the Universe has more to offer than we could ever imagine. Accept change, let go and positive things will come your way.
- Victory or defeat, worldly success or otherwise, it is all the same; for when we transition beyond the earthly realm, the only thing that really matters is how we treated and related to others.

Chapter 14

The Physical Body: Its Purpose, Care and Demise

What is the purpose of our physical body and its relationship to us?

We are not merely our bodies. Our bodies contain our soul-consciousness or life-force which, as we have seen in Chapter 12, is eternal. The physical body itself is perishable and has been described in the *Tibetan Book of the Dead: The Main Verses of the Six Bardos* as a compound of flesh and blood which is nothing more than "a transitory illusion." However, our body is much more than that and has been described in the Christian *New Testament* as "a temple of the Holy Spirit within you" (1 Corinthians chapter 6 verse 19). According to some faiths like Christianity, Islam, Baha'i and Sikhism, God is immanent or indwelling within each of us as a Divine spark. As the body is a Divine sanctuary, it should be well cared for, maintained and respected and not subject to excesses or over-indulgence. In relation to Eastern faiths, Buddhism perceives the body and Earthly life as facilitating a dispelling of ignorance and a growth towards eventual enlightenment in the context of limitless physical incarnations in various life forms. According to Buddhist beliefs, what we call life is a combination of physical and mental energies which are constantly changing. What we refer to as death is the total non-functioning of the physical body. But certain mental energies – the desire or will to continue to exist and to be, to become more and more, and to experience worldly pleasures – do not cease with the death of the physical body but continue to manifest in other forms, producing rebirth in the form of another life. As long as this craving to be and become continues, the cycle of continuity (*samsara*) goes on until this craving is extinguished through wisdom which perceives the Ultimate Reality, Truth or *Nirvana*. And Hinduism perceives the body as affording an opportunity to burn off or consume accumulated negative *karma* over countless rebirths, eventually leading to self-realization or enlightenment.

The authors of various near death experience accounts utilize a variety of descriptions of the function or purpose of the human body. The physical body has been described, for example, as the soul's prison for the duration of our Earthly lifetime. It has also been described as the soul's shell or shelter or its temporary home or resting-place. And reminiscent of Buddhism and Hinduism, others describe the body as an Earthly vessel which is borrowed temporarily to enable our soul-consciousness to experience Earthly life and all that such life entails, and to learn and grow from that experience, drawing upon positive energies and avoiding negative energies.

As the physical body is transient and perishable, what, then, is the spiritual significance of its death?

Many fear death and are so preoccupied with the prospect of death that they fail to live their life to the fullest. But as the NDE accounts tell us, although death is the extinction of our body, our soul-consciousness is eternal and continues on lifetime after lifetime. There is no reason then to fear the death of our body. In fact, many of the NDE accounts essentially observe that rather than something to fear, death of the body is something to look forward to. In reality, death is an illusion or, rather, a poor descriptor of what actually happens.

The death of our body has been beautifully and elegantly described in some of the NDE accounts. Basically it is the separation or disconnection of the soul-consciousness from the body. Upon death, it is said that we leave behind our Earthly identity, our physical pain and suffering and our Earthly cares and anxieties. Death is a shedding of our physical existence and a transition of our soul-consciousness to a spiritually-based existence in which our energy assumes a new form and our soul transitions to heightened and more acute thought, perception, awareness and consciousness. Our death in the physical Earthly plane re-births us into the spiritual realms which have been described by some of the NDE authors as the Ultimate Reality in which the true nature of all things may be more readily recognized. Our births in the physical and spiritual realms have indeed been described by one author as sacred events. According to the NDE accounts (which are corroborated by some scriptural references which follow), the death of our body is the leaving behind of our temporary home and a return to our real or true home for rest, self-assessment and debriefing of the soul before its next physical rebirth or incarnation. It is a natural continuation of an eternal process of our spiritual evolution towards God/Source.

Scriptural References
Baha'i
I have placed in you the essence of My Light. Therefore be illumined by it and seek no one else but Me.
(Of the Light: Words of Wisdom from the Supreme Pen of Baha'u'llah)

Moderation is desirable in every affair.
(Tablet of Baha'u'llah: Words of Paradise)

Buddhism
Restraint in all things is good.
(The Dhammapada chapter 25 (The Bhikshu/Mendicant) verse 361)

Over and over again living beings are born, they age, die, pass on to a new life, and are reborn! Greed and dark delusion obscure their sight, and they are blind from birth.... Beginning with ignorance, they progress to old age and death, and, beginning with the cessation of ignorance, they lead to the cessation of birth, old age, death and all kinds of ill.
(The Enlightenment of the Buddha: Buddhacarita)

It is because of a mind at peace that certain beings, when the body breaks up, after death arise again in the happy bourn, in the heaven-world (one who does not return to rebirth goes to a heaven and there attains *nirvana*).
(The Way to Nirvana: Khuddaka Nikaya, Itivuttaka)

Christianity
Behold, the Kingdom of God is within you.
(Luke chapter 17 verse 21)

Take heed to yourselves (be cautious), lest at any time your hearts be overcharged with surfeiting (excess in eating) and drunkenness and cares of this life.
(Luke chapter 21 verse 34)

Do you not know that your body is the temple of the Holy Spirit which is in you, which you have of God, and you are not your own?
(1 Corinthians chapter 6 verse 19)

Every person who strives for ... (self-) mastery is temperate (exercises moderation) in all things.
(1 Corinthians chapter 9 verse 25)

There are heavenly bodies and earthly bodies; and the splendour of the heavenly bodies is one thing, the splendour of the earthly, another.... What is sown in the earth as a perishable thing is raised imperishable ... sown as an animal body, it is raised as a spiritual body. If there is such a thing as an animal body, there is also a spiritual body ... the perishable cannot possess immortality.... This perishable being must be clothed with the imperishable, and what is mortal must be clothed with immortality. And when our mortality has been clothed with immortality, then the saying of Scripture will come true: "Death is swallowed up; victory is won!" "O Death, where is your victory? O Death, where is your sting?"
(1 Corinthians chapter 15 verses 40–55)

Hinduism

The human body is the temple of God. One who kindles the light of awareness within gets true light.
(Rig Veda)

Cleanliness (external cleanliness of the body and internal purity of the soul).
(Saintly Virtue No. 24 of those endowed with a Divine Nature: Bhagavad-Gita chapter 16 verses 1–3)

One should practice ... self-restraint (*damyata*).
(The Three Da's: Brhadaranyaka Upanisad)

Let one not, out of desire (for enjoyments), attach oneself to sensual pleasures and let one carefully obviate an excessive attachment to them.
(The Laws of Manu: Manava-dharma-sastra chapter 4 verses 1–18)

Kala (Time) is no one's friend and no one's enemy: when the effect of his acts in a former existence, by which his present existence is caused, has expired, (Time) snatches a man away forcibly. He will not die before his time has come, even though he has been pierced by a thousand shafts; he will not live after his time is out, even though he has only been touched by the point of a blade of kusa grass.... As the body of a mortal undergoes infancy, youth, and old age, even so will it be transformed into another body.... As a man puts on new clothes in this world, throwing aside those which he formerly wore, even so the (soul) of man puts on new bodies, which are in accordance with his acts (in a former life) ... (the soul) is imperishable, perpetual, unchanging, immovable, without beginning.... Knowing the (soul) of man to be such, you must not grieve (for the destruction of his body).

(Vaisnava-dharma-sastra chapter 20 verses 39–53) '

The *atman* (individual soul/self) can give no reason for grief, for it is immortal. One does not mourn over the embodied *atman* when it passes from one stage (life or existence) to another. But the immortal *atman* is subject to beginningless *karma*, and is, for this reason, created conjointly with bodies that are determined by its various *karma*. By means of these bodies the *atman* performs acts which are prescribed by the *sastras* to each station and stage of life ... to be released from their bondage to these bodies. So the *atman* has inevitably contacts with objects through the senses of their bodies and these contacts cause sensations of pain and pleasure.... If one is persistent, one will be able to endure them, for they are transient by nature and will cease to exist as soon as the evil which has caused the *atman's* bondage has been annihilated ... the immortality of the *atman* and the mortality of the body can cause no grief.... The entity *atman*, which is a spiritual body, pervades the non-spiritual entity (the

body) which is different from the *atman*. Hence it follows that the *atman* is subtler (of higher vibration) than all other beings which necessarily must be grosser if the *atman* is to pervade them.... The body is perishable because it serves to enable its innate *atman* to undergo its accumulated *karma* ... grief for the *atman* results from a misconception. The innate *atman* cannot be destroyed, even if its body be destroyed.
(Ramanuja on the Atman and Body: Commentary to the Bhagavad-Gita)

Islam

It is better for you to practice self-restraint.
(The Women chapter 4 verse 25)

He is God; there is no God but He (Allah) ... to Him shall you (your soul) be returned.
(The Story chapter 28 verse 70)

Everyone shall taste (physical) death. Then to Us (God) you (your soul) shall be returned.
(The Spider chapter 29 verse 57)

God knows what the soul whispers and God is nearer than the jugular vein.
(Qaf chapter 50 verse 16)

Jainism

The soul, which suffers for its carelessness, is driven about in the round of rebirth (successive physical incarnations) by its good and bad *karma*.
(The Simile of the Leaf: Uttaradhyayana)

Living beings of sinful actions (producing negative *karma*) are born again and again in ever-recurring births.... But by the cessation of *karma*, living beings will reach in due time a pure state.... The pious obtain purity, and the pure stand firmly in the Law: the soul afterwards reaches the highest *Nirvana*.... Leave off the causes of sin, acquire patience! You will rise to the upper regions after having left this body of clay.
(Living Beings and the Round of Rebirth: Uttaradhyayana)

One should practice self-control.
(Uttaradhyayana: Thirty-First Lecture: Mode of Life)

Sikhism
By His (God's) order bodies are produced.... By His order souls are infused into them.... By His order some obtain their reward; by His order others must ever wander in transmigration. All are subject to His order; none is exempt from it.
(Guru Nanak's Japji)

Human life grows shorter every day ... (therefore) arrange your affairs.... They whom God awakens and causes to drink the essence of His word, know the story of the Ineffable Embrace for which you have come into the world and God ... will dwell in your heart. You shall find a home with comfort and peace in God's own palace and not return again in this world.
(From the Sohila: Guru Arjan)

The Lord ... gives life to all the world, His light shines in all life born.
(Spiritual Marriage: The Bara Mah)

The One God is in every place.... He is in the soul and the soul is in Him.
(Hymn by Guru Arjan)

Thou, O God, the one Supreme Being, are fully contained in every heart.
(From the Rahiras: Guru Ram Das)

Taoism

Not to desire the things of sense (of the five senses) is to know the freedom of spirituality; and to desire is to learn the limitations of matter.
(Lao Tzu, Tao Te Ching (What is the Tao) chapter 1)

All things are in process, rising and returning. Plants come to blossom, but only to return to the root. Returning to the root (God/the Source/the true nature of our soul) is like seeking tranquillity; it is moving towards its destiny. To move towards destiny is like eternity. To know eternity is enlightenment.... The decay of the body is not to be feared.
(Lao Tzu, Tao Te Ching (Returning to the Source) chapter 16)

Those who seek to grasp it, will lose it. Therefore the wise (person) practices moderation, abandoning pleasure, extravagance and indulgence.
(Lao Tzu, Tao Te Ching (Not Forcing Things (*Wu Wei*)) chapter 29)

Life is a going forth; death (of the body) is a returning home (to God/the Source).
(Lao Tzu. Tao Te Ching (Esteem Life) chapter 50)

In worshipping Heaven, nothing surpasses moderation ... (possessing moderation) is like having deep roots and a strong stem.
(Lao Tzu, Tao Te Ching (To Keep Tao) chapter 59)

Zoroastrianism

No pleasure but has its concomitant pain ... let the avoidance of excess in everything be most particularly inculcated ...

(over-indulgences) encourage the most deadly sins and the soul so indulging will most assuredly be cut off from Heaven ... the indulgence of our passions brings no pleasure of long duration, or impresses any good sentiment on the heart.
(The Vision of Arda-Viraf)

NDE Accounts

The Nature of the Physical Body:

- Your body is an earthly vessel which you are temporarily borrowing. Therefore respect and treat it well.
- You are much more than your physical body.
- Our physical body is but a shell or house to contain our soul during its Earthly journey.
- I understood that my body was my shell for my time on this earth.
- Our body and spirit are one. The body is the soul's container or receptacle. Our body entraps our soul in the earthly plane.
- The body is the soul's prison.
- Our human body is connected to higher vibrational levels. It is dense, heavy and limiting.
- The physical body is a vessel that enables our higher consciousness to inhabit it in order to learn and grow from our Earthly experiences.
- Your physical body and Earthly name are temporarily borrowed so that you may play your role in this transient play called Life. Upon completion of our role, we leave both behind.
- Our Earthly life is like a caterpillar. In human form, we are limited and move slowly with our cumbersome bodies. On death, we shed the chrysalis (transitional state) and take on a more beautiful form like a butterfly.
- God resides within us; within our heart, soul and spirit.

- God is within each of us and speaks to us within.
- God and eternity are within you.

Death of the Physical Body:

- Death is the separation of the soul from the physical body. It is a release from its Earthly prison.
- Do not fear death as it is illusory.
- Life does not end when we die.
- Death is not the end, but only the beginning of something more glorious than we can ever imagine.
- Death is not a finality; rather, it is a transition from one realm or state to another.
- Our souls never die.
- When our body dies, our soul-consciousness does not die.
- Death is a natural part of life and continuing consciousness.
- Fear of death is human error. Our souls are eternal and thus continue on.
- There is no need to fear physical death as your consciousness survives it. Your death in the physical realm re-births you into the spiritual realm.
- People fear death, like a thief in the night no one can avoid. I know this to be farthest from the truth. Within death, there is a complete cleansing of the spirit, a washing away of our realities of the flesh and an awakening of the spirit to truths no language can begin to describe. Death is a beginning, not a destination.
- I no longer fear death as I know from my (out-of-body) experience that my soul survives my bodily death.
- Death is a shedding of our physical/material existence for a spiritually-based existence.
- The death of the physical body is our spirit shedding its earthly skin.

- Death is the soul's transition of experiential existences to other planes or realms.
- While the process leading up to the death of the body may involve pain and suffering, the moment of death, in which we surrender to the call to return to our real home, is painless. Our soul simply transitions to a new and different realm.
- Physical death is not the end but a change or transition or a movement forward. We come from "the other side" and return there when we shed our physical body. Our energy assumes a new form.
- Death is like being extricated from a tight confined space. It is a leaving behind of heaviness, density and slowness. The soul's vibrations increase, allowing it an expanded consciousness, freedom of movement and experience of Love.
- What humans refer to as physical death is one of the Creator's greatest gifts, used for the transition of your spirit into higher realms.
- Death is a process of continuing our spiritual evolutionary journey. Our births into the earthly realm and our births into the spiritual realm are sacred events.
- Physical death is a natural continuum of the soul's eternal transitioning journey.
- There is no such thing as death; demise of the physical body is merely an escape or release therefrom for the soul and its transition to a higher state of consciousness.
- Physical death is a doorway to Home.
- The other side of the veil is our true home. Death is not the end but only a transition to our true home.
- Death is returning home, an awakening or heightened awareness.

- Death is a returning Home for debriefing and reprogramming.
- When you discard your body, you discard your pain and earthly cares.
- On death our soul disconnects from our physical body and no longer suffers pain and anguish.
- When your soul leaves your body, you become detached from the earthly realm and become an emotionally neutral and distant observer of events therein.
- I was not at all worried about the fact that I was dead. Knowing that I had died seemed totally irrelevant and unimportant. I was not even slightly curious or interested in the body I had left behind.
- Each of us dies at the right moment. It may not seem so in the Earthly realm but it is so in the spiritual realms.
- By accepting the inevitability and purpose of one's physical death, we become serene and peaceful.
- I knew – with total certainty – that everything was evolving exactly the way it should and that the ultimate destiny of every living being is to return to the Source, the Light, Pure Love.
- We all get our day of atonement (at-one-ment) when our physical body dies and our soul meets the Light.
- The part that is TRULY me had left my body and was in a place of pure light – a warm, gentle, loving fog had enveloped me and was me. All of my pain and trauma disappeared. I was welcomed by three Beings of Light with the most incredible love, acceptance and compassion.

Chapter 15

Free Will

Free Will is a precious gift bestowed upon each of us by God. We have the freedom or autonomy to make decisions for ourselves which affect us in our daily living, ranging from personal health and well-being issues to our jobs, careers, relationships with others and what we believe or choose not to believe. As such, Free Will plays a most significant part in our lives and how we choose to live our life – our particular life experiences are chosen by us. As some of those who have undergone a near death experience observe, God honors and respects all of the choices and decisions we make for ourselves but we remain responsible for them at the soul level (which will later be discussed in Chapter 20 entitled "Self-Reflection, Acknowledgment and Enlightenment"). And according to the Abrahamic religions (Judaism, Christianity and Islam), Humanity has been given God's Law but each of us is free to either accept and act on it or to reject it.

Why are each of us granted Free Will? A domestic or family analogy may assist. As loving and caring parents who want the best for their children, we allow them increasing autonomy and independence to make their own decisions and choices as they mature and their decision-making capacity evolves. However, we know as parents that they will sometimes make mistakes (as we all do), but we hope and indeed expect that they will acknowledge, accept responsibility for, and learn from their mistakes and thereby grow and mature into responsible adults. Similarly, God allows us to find our way or to blunder through life by letting us make our own choices when we reach the proverbial fork in the road. The choices we make either help us to achieve our soul's mission in life or take us further away from it. Sometimes we must fall and pick ourselves up again for our souls to learn and grow. And sometimes sadly, we do not learn and forget why we are here and what we are supposed to do. But making mistakes and suffering the consequences therefrom help us to learn and evolve and align with our Earthly mission.

God does not want to force us to love Him or to force us to strive after Divine virtue or righteousness. Of course, He wants such striving but to force us to do so would not be genuine, authentic, honest or pure. God wants us to be spontaneous, joyful and genuine rather than grudging. He loves us so dearly and unconditionally that He allows us to make a choice between growing towards Him or falling away from Him. Free Will can, of course, be exercised for positive or negative purposes or, to put it into the language of the Abrahamic religions and Eastern metaphysical philosophy respectively, good or evil or wise/ enlightened/awakened or ignorant/lacking in skill. Negative energy, evil and ignorance do not exist in the higher spiritual realms but are necessary in the Earthly realm to enable our souls to make important Free Will choices. Our cumulative life choices will either facilitate a growth and evolution of our soul-consciousness towards God or a falling away from the Light and consequent misalignment with our Earthly mission.

Free Will is vital to pursuing and succeeding in our Earthly life's mission and in facilitating our ascendance into the higher spiritual realms. Our purpose here on Earth is to grow towards the Divine but we can just as easily fall away depending on how wisely or ignorantly we have exercised our gift of Free Will. For those who actively pursue and live by the positive energy of the Universe, there is great reward; for those who choose to pursue negative energy, there is forgiveness and an opportunity for redemption (see Chapters 8 and 9 for a discussion of, and observations on, positive and negative energy). The exercise of our gift of Free Will in such a manner as to resist negative energy and utilize positive energy in the living of our life facilitates an elevation and expansion of our soul-consciousness.

Many of us today perceive ourselves to be "victims" of life and what it throws at us, and this term seems to be gaining increasing currency in contemporary discourse. Admittedly there are many things and circumstances in our life which lie largely beyond our control. But as a number of those authors who have recorded their near death experience attest to, all too often we are also victims of the way in which we have exercised our Free Will through unwise or ignorant decision-making and choices which have drawn too much on negative rather than positive energy.

What follows are relevant scriptural passages on the gift of Free Will as well as some of the observations and insights made thereon by the authors of those IANDS written accounts studied.

Scriptural References
Buddhism

All conditioned (created) things are impermanent. Work out your own salvation with diligence.
(The Buddha's Last Words)

Purity and impurity depend on oneself. No one can purify another.
(The Dhammapada chapter 12 (Self) verse 165)

The wise (person) who, as if holding a pair of scales, chooses what is good and avoids what is evil, is indeed a sage.
(The Dhammapada chapter 19 (The Just) verse 269)

Christianity

And whosoever will, let them take the water of life freely.
(Revelation chapter 22 verse 17)

Confucianism

The Truth must be genuinely and earnestly realized by each person on their own.
(Chu Hsi on the Great Ultimate: Chu tzu ch'uan-shu)

Islam

There is no compulsion in religion; the right path has been distinguished from the wrong path.
(The Cow chapter 2 verse 256)

The Truth has come from your Lord: let those who wish to believe in it do so, and let those who wish to reject it do so.
(The Cave chapter 18 verse 29)

Judaism

I call Heaven and Earth to record this day against you, that I have set before you life and death, blessing and cursing: therefore choose life, that both you and your seed may live.
(Deuteronomy chapter 30 verses 19–20)

You may choose for yourself, for it is given unto you.
(Moses chapter 3 verse 17)

NDE Accounts

- God is unconditional love and gives us the gift of free will to make our own choices.
- Free will to create our own earthly reality is the greatest gift we are given.
- We are given opportunities in life and we have free will to make choices.
- Our experiences are what we choose through exercising our free will.

- Life is a journey or adventure for our soul. Through the exercise of our gift of Free Will, we can make of it whatever we will.
- The experience we call life is only transitory. It is a place of preparation, of choices, of opportunities to grow.
- I understood from the Light that I was here (on Earth) to learn and to grow (should that be what I chose to take from my earthly experiences).
- We are here on Earth by choice to fulfill our soul's life purpose. We are unique and precious to God. We are only expected to love, and be of service to, others, through exercise of Free Will.
- Your purpose is what you say it is. Your mission is what you set for yourself. Your life is what you create for yourself and no one will stand in judgment but you.
- A Life Review is re-living and an opportunity to consider what our soul has learned from the incarnation's experiences and interactions. There is no judgment or condemnation. Only we judge ourselves from a perspective outside ourselves with clear-sighted vision. We discover how profound an impact seemingly insignificant actions had on others and how the exercise of our free will and decision-making ripples outward to countless others. And the hurt we inflict on others in turn causes them to inflict hurt on yet others that we could never have anticipated.
- One's entire life is witnessed (during the so-called Life Review) from a third party observer's point of view, from the soul's point of view and that of those who were affected by the soul's acts and deeds. The soul feels the feelings and emotions of those who were affected by the soul's positive and negative conduct. The soul gains the perspective of the humans who were affected by the soul's choices. Even the soul's seemingly innocent choices can have implications beyond which we could ever have

imagined. It therefore matters deeply what choices we as humans make in exercise of our gift of free will.

- Each of us has the power to change our course through free will.
- We determine our own path by exercising our free will and making decisions when arriving at forks in our personal path.
- Everything you have done and all you have been through were to prepare you for the juncture in your life right now. We are free to choose from among many forks in our path. But with such freedom comes responsibility, so choose wisely.
- Life is not a series of coincidences but of choices made, the consequences for which we remain responsible for at the soul level.
- God honors all choices we make pursuant to our free will. He will not veto our choices but we remain accountable to our Higher Selves for those choices.
- Each soul has the free will to choose its own destiny, to choose between positive and negative energies, but the universal laws are such that the soul has to face the effects of what it chooses.
- Human free will is that part of our soul that is able to render positive service to the Universe if it so chooses. That free will can also be exercised for negative purposes.
- The gift of free will is a great gift, but decisions should be made from our soul heart to secure the greatest good overall.
- It is our privilege to be granted Free Will. We decide and make choices. So how then can we feel that we are a victim?
- Do you consider yourself a victim? Aren't we all? Focus rather on what you want going forward and your past will fall away. You are the designer and author of your destiny.

Chapter 16

The Inner Life: Our Conscience and Intuition

The mind is very powerful. Our thoughts create our individual reality. Our life is what our thoughts make it (from *Meditations* by Roman Emperor Marcus Aurelius). As we think, so we are. If we wish to create a better personal reality for ourselves, we must purify the upstream (our thoughts and thought processes) in order to cleanse the downstream (our words and actions).

Possessing and exercising an inner conscience involves the internal and intuitive recognition of the moral or ethical quality of right and wrong (or positive and negative) concerning one's actions, omissions and motives. It is paying heed to that quiet but persistent and uncompromising inner voice, the Divine spark within us, when conducting oneself (or contemplating conducting oneself) contrary to religious desiderata and Divine Law or otherwise behaving inappropriately or unskillfully or beyond the bounds of propriety. We must strive to listen and pay heed to the voice of our soul. These inner whisperings must not be suppressed as our Higher Self wants the best for us and our spiritual development. An inner conscience aligns us with, or returns us to, the Divine path and moves us forward towards the Light. And we must also trust our intuition or instincts as that inexplicable but confident knowing may well be based on knowledge gained previously by the soul-consciousness in the spiritual realms. Therefore seek and trust the inner and do not be distracted by the outer; true beauty shines from deep within the soul.

Scriptural References
Buddhism

All that we are is the result of what we have thought: it is founded on our thoughts, it is made up of our thoughts.
(The Dhammapada chapter 1 (The Twin-Verses) verse 2)

A controlled mind brings happiness.
(The Dhammapada chapter 3 (Thought) verse 35)

Watchful of speech, well restrained in mind, do no evil with the body.
(The Dhammapada chapter 20 (The Way) verse 281)

Good is restraint in thought. Restraint in all things is good.
(The Dhammapada chapter 25 (The Bhikshu/Mendicant) verse 361)

The resting place for the mind is in the heart.
(Anonymous Buddhist monk)

Christianity

The Kingdom of God is within you.
(Luke chapter 17 verse 21)

Have always a conscience void of offence towards God and towards others.
(Acts chapter 24 verse 16)

Confucianism

The feeling of shame (produced by the exercise of one's conscience) is the beginning of righteousness.
(The Innateness of the Four Great Virtues: Mencius)

If you lead the people through virtue and regulate them by the laws of propriety, then they will have a sense of shame (be pricked by their own conscience) and will attain goodness.
(Analects)

The feeling of right and wrong is the beginning of wisdom.
(The Innateness of the Four Great Virtues: Mencius)

Have no wrong (unethical and anti-social) thoughts.
(Analects)

The mind is the master of the body.
(The Investigation of the Mind: Yang-ming's Conversations with Huang I-fang)

Hinduism

Modesty. (*Hrih* means a sense of guilt or shame in performing actions contrary to the injunctions of scriptures and society.)
(Saintly Virtue No. 19 of those endowed with a Divine Nature: Bhagavad-Gita chapter 16 verses 1–3)

If one inquires "Who am I?", the mind will go back to its source; and the thought that arose will become quiescent. With repeated practice in this manner, the mind will develop the skill to stay in its source.... Not letting the mind go out, but retaining it in the Heart is what is called "inwardness" (*antarmukha*).... Thus, when the mind stays in the Heart, the "I" which is the source of all thoughts will go, and the Self (soul-consciousness) which ever exists will shine.
(The Teachings of Bhagavan Sri Ramana Maharshi: Who Am I? (Nan Yar?))

Islam

If you obey and fear (are mindful of) God, He will grant you *Furqan* (a conscience or criterion to judge between right and wrong).
(The Spoils chapter 8 verse 29)

Jainism

The wise restrain their senses. They should do no harm to anybody, neither by thoughts, nor words, nor acts.
(Sutrakrtanga: Book 1 Eleventh Lecture: The Path)

Judaism

As I think in my heart, so am I.
(Proverbs chapter 23 verse 7)

Taoism

The wise attend to the inner significance of things and do not concern themselves with outward appearances. Therefore they ignore matter (materialism and worldliness) and seek the spirit (spiritual treasures of the heart).
(Lao Tzu, Tao Te Ching (Avoiding Desire) chapter 12)

To the mind that is still, the whole universe surrenders.
(Lao Tzu)

We cannot see our reflection in running water. It is only in still water that we can see.
(Taoist proverb)

Zen Buddhism

Do not follow the ideas of others, but learn to listen to the voice within yourself. Your body and mind will become clear and you will realize the unity (interconnectedness) of all things.
(Dogen)

Be a master of the mind, not mastered by the mind.
(Zen proverb)

Zoroastrianism

I praise the well-thought, well-spoken, well-performed thoughts, words and works.... I abandon all evil thoughts, words and works.
(The Creed)

NDE Accounts

- The Truth lies within you.
- The answers you seek are not to be found outside of you but all lie within you. Deconstruct all of the social and religious constructs you have accumulated during your lifetime and tune into the infinite and eternal Divine energy source within you.
- Unlock the inner to rest and repose in eternity.
- Never lose your conscience.
- Listen to your conscience, the gentle whisperings of your higher self and God within.
- Since my near-death experience, I rely on my inner voice more often than I do reason and logic.
- Trust your instincts, follow your heart and soul, listen to your inner true self, live your life in alignment with your life's purpose and share your light and love.
- In the spirit world, understandings will come to you which you have always known but temporarily forgot while in the physical realm. Therefore, trust your intuition as that inexplicable knowing is based on knowledge derived in the spiritual realm (between Earthly incarnations).
- Do not strive for the outer things; strive first for the inner things.

- Feel and see with your heart. Perceive and consider important what is on the inside of a person; not on what is outside.
- Your thoughts and your feelings create your life and your own reality.
- Your thoughts instantly create your reality.
- Cleanse your thought process. Thoughts are very powerful; and as you think, so you are. They have creative effects in this world and in the Universe.
- What we think about, we bring about.
- We become what we think about.
- You attract to yourself whatever the thoughts you have inside you.
- A person's inner being is pre-speech and is more basic than emotions. It is your source of personal power and is your real self-identity. An adjustment to a person's inner being, however slight, can generate profound changes.
- Real beauty shines from deep within the soul. Unlike physical beauty which fades with time, real beauty comes from within and never fades. It is internal and eternal. Contentedness cannot be found without; it can only come from within our spiritual heart.

Chapter 17

Living in the Present Moment:
The Eternal Now

In Chapter 7 it was noted that many of those who crossed over to the Other Side reported in their written accounts that Time as we know and experience this concept on Earth does not exist in the Higher Realms, where the past and future do not exist in a linear sense but everything is happening now. Eternity is one second and one second an eternity. On Earth we are used to the concept of linear or sequential time in which we all have a past, a present and a future. But this observation on Time from beyond the veil may indeed be very instructive as an injunction on how we can live our lives more fully and usefully in this realm.

Many of us are too busy contemplating and planning for the future or mulling over past mistakes, regrets and lost opportunities to recognize and appreciate the beauty, wonder and awe of the present moment. Since we cannot undo our past and have only limited and tenuous control over the future, and acknowledging the absolute impermanence of things which are visible to the eye, it is necessary to rejoice in the preciousness and fullness of the present moment.

Maintaining a clear and focused mind, undistracted by misgivings over the past and anxieties concerning the future, is a theme predominant within the Buddhist and Jain traditions, although it is also found within the Abrahamic religions. The Buddhist concept of right mindfulness is the ability to maintain constant and complete awareness of, or attentiveness to, what one is doing, thinking and feeling from moment to moment, unencumbered by reflections of the past and anxieties about the future. One must fully, simply and calmly concentrate on the task at hand, completing each task one at a time. Daily tasks may therefore be undertaken wholeheartedly and vigorously rather than superficially and distractedly. In Jainism, the past has already ceased to exist; the future has not yet been born. As past memories may contaminate our future outlook, it is better to seek refuge in the reality of the present moment. It is in the here and now that we must reconcile ourselves to our past by forgiving ourselves and others; it is in the here and now that we relearn everything from moment to moment and evolve and shape our destiny. In Islam, mindfulness is a spiritual state in which our mind and heart are conscious of the Divine in the present moment as opposed to a state of wandering, inner dialogue or forgetfulness.

Our exclusive focus must therefore be an awareness of the present moment (the so-called "Eternal Now"). It has been said that the highest nobility lies in taming or stilling your own mind (Tibetan Buddhist Atisha). Mindfulness penetrates through to the reality underlying worldly appearances and delusions. Through mindfulness and meditation, we free the mind and awaken to the appreciation and joy of our existence. Therefore, enjoy to the fullest each precious fleeting moment of this life, as what has passed may well never happen again. Let every moment be a new beginning (Zen proverb).

Scriptural References
Buddhism
Do not pursue the past. Do not lose yourself in the future. The past no longer is. The future is yet to come. Looking very deeply at life as it is here and now, one dwells in stability and freedom. (Bhaddekaratta Sutta)

It is good to tame the mind, which is difficult to restrain and flighty, rushing wherever it lists. A tamed mind brings happiness.
(The Dhammapada chapter 3 (Thought) verse 35)

Do not dwell in the past. Do not dream of the future. Concentrate the mind on the present moment.
(The Buddha)

The resting place for the mind is in the heart.
(Anonymous Buddhist monk)

The secret of health for both mind and body is not to mourn for the past, nor to worry about the future, but to live the present moment wisely and earnestly.
(Buddhist teaching)

Christianity

Take no thought (worry or anxiety) about what shall we eat or what shall we drink or what clothes shall we wear.... But seek first the kingdom of God and His righteousness and all these things shall be added unto you. Take therefore no thought for tomorrow, for tomorrow will have worries of its own. Sufficient for each day is its own trouble.
(Matthew chapter 6 verses 31, 33–4)

Do not be conformed to this world, but be transformed by the renewal of your mind.
(Romans chapter 12 verse 2)

Do not lose heart. Though our outer self is wasting away, our inner self is being renewed day by day.
(2 Corinthians chapter 4 verse 16)

You do not know what tomorrow will bring. For what is your life? For you are a mist that appears for a little time and then vanishes.
(James chapter 4 verse 14)

Confucianism
The mind is the master of the body.
(The Investigation of the Mind: Wang Yang-ming's Conversations with Huang I-fang)

Hinduism
Look to this day, for it is life, the very breath of life. In its brief course lie all the realities of your existence; the bliss of growth, the glory of action, the splendor of beauty. For yesterday is only a dream, and tomorrow is but a vision. But today, well lived, makes every yesterday a dream of happiness, and every tomorrow a vision of hope. Look well, therefore, to this day.
(Ancient Sanskrit)

When the mind stays in the Heart, the "I" which is the source of all thoughts will go.
(The Teachings of Bhagavan Sri Ramana Maharshi: Who Am I? (Nan Yar?))

Islam
Never say of anything, "I am going to do such and such thing tomorrow." Except (with the saying), "If God wills!"
(The Cave chapter 18 verses 23–4)

Surely in this there is a reminder for one who has a (mindful) heart, whoever listens attentively (those who are fully present in a situation and listen to and contemplate what is being said and internalize it into their inner being/essence).
(Qaf chapter 50 verse 37)

Judaism

This is the day that the Lord has made; let us rejoice and be glad in it.

(Psalm 118 verse 24)

Remember not the former things, nor consider the things of old. Behold, I am doing a new thing; now it springs forth.

(Isaiah chapter 43 verses 18–19)

(Do not be too certain) of tomorrow; for you do not know what a day may bring forth.

(Proverbs chapter 27 verse 1)

Taoism

To the mind that is still, the whole universe surrenders.

(Lao Tzu)

We cannot see our reflection in running water. It is only in still water that we can see.

(Taoist proverb)

Zen Buddhism

Do one thing at a time. Do it slowly and deliberately. Do it completely.

(The Zen Manifesto)

Relearn everything. Let every moment be a new beginning.

(Zen proverb)

Be a master of the mind, not mastered by the mind.

(Zen proverb)

NDE Accounts

- Live in the present moment.
- Live in the moment. The future and past are now.
- Live completely in the moment or in the now or in the flow.
- Do not be so concerned with planning the future or worrying about the past that you are forgoing the joys of living fully in the present moment.
- There is no past. There is no future. There is only now.
- Every moment matters. Therefore live mindfully and fully in the present moment.
- Make one second into an eternity and an eternity into a single second.
- Do not harbor any expectations for if you do, you are surely bound to be ultimately disappointed. Live each day as fully and preciously as if it was your last.
- Live each day to the fullest as if it was your last.
- Feel the perfection of every moment of your life which has led you to the present moment.
- Death is an exhale which is not followed by an inhale. Reflect on the value of your breath in sustaining life and in meditative mindfulness of the present moment. Your breath is all that stands between life and physical death. Therefore be conscious of, and in, your breathing.
- Be helpful, present in the moment and a good listener.

Chapter 18

Universal Knowledge and Understanding

It has been said that they who know themselves know God.

Knowledge and understanding exist at varying levels. According to Buddhism, there are two main types of understanding – what is generally referred to as accumulated knowledge or memory and an intellectual comprehension of a subject based on existing information and data sets (what is referred to as *anubodha*); as opposed to a deeper and more penetrative understanding which perceives a phenomenon or thing as it is in its true nature (*pativedha*).

While human knowledge and understanding of the seen material physical realm we call Earth have been advancing and accumulating for millennia, we are only now on the threshold of a greater and more profound understanding of the unseen spiritual realms and dimensions. As a Qur'anic verse has observed, how impossible it is for humanity to understand, beyond the most basic and rudimentary level, the spiritual realms, as humanity has been given only a little knowledge thereof by the Creator (The Journey by Night chapter 17 verse 85). We are squarely located within the realm of metaphysics – study and research into that which cannot be learned, at least at this point in history, through objective study of material reality; a postulated reality outside of human sense perception. But this may well be changing with recent advances in science (particularly quantum mechanics physics) and medical and scientific research into the near death experience phenomenon. All Divine knowledge of the unseen realms is imparted by God to humanity as and when He wills.

Divine understanding is not the same as human understanding. A prodigious gulf separates them; only the former can enlighten or awaken or remind the soul. Buddhism teaches that in order to fully and truly understand, we have to become one with what we want to understand. Knowledge of the Divine is understanding (Proverbs chapter 9 verse 10) and those who seek God understand all things (Proverbs chapter 28 verse 5). Understanding is knowledge of, and insight into, the Divine. Deep or penetrative understanding is the capacity or ability to recognize and comprehend the Truth, the Dharma or the Tao (as the case may be). Understanding in the Buddhist *pativedha* sense is perceiving the way things actually are as opposed to the way we perceive them to be; observing each thing or phenomenon in its true nature as it actually and objectively is, rather than through the prism of material illusion (described by the Hindu term *maya-nivrtti*), the attachment of labels or names, or through the cultural-religious filter of one's lifelong accumulated individual preconceptions and conditioning. Understanding extends to comprehending and realizing our highest vision of our soul's potential (self-knowledge). Those who understand themselves, and know who they truly are, are enlightened (Tao Te Ching).

Many of those who have undergone an NDE report that once outside the body, they receive instantaneous knowledge and awareness. They use various terms to describe what happens to them in this regard, including "osmosis," "downloading," "infusion," "plugging in," or "wired in." They become aware of how the seen physical and unseen spiritual worlds operate and interact with each other and gain an instantaneous understanding of conceptually difficult, complex and challenging matters that would take much longer on Earth to absorb and comprehend. Some report that the received knowledge is that which has always been known by the soul-consciousness but temporarily forgotten during its Earthly incarnation. A certain level of knowingness or omniscience is attained whereby certainty and proof henceforward replace trust and faith. I no longer believe because I now know (referring, for example, to the existence of God/the Source, Heaven, Beings of Light, the purpose of our life on Earth and reincarnation).

Scriptural References
Baha'i
The root of all knowledge is the knowledge of God.
(Of Knowledge: Words of Wisdom from the Supreme Pen of Baha'u'llah)

Buddhism
The eye was born, knowledge was born, wisdom was born, science was born, light was born. (The Buddha, with reference to his own Enlightenment).
(The First Sermon: Vinaya, Mahavagga)

Christianity
The Lord will give you understanding in all things.
(2 Timothy chapter 2 verse 7)

If any of you lacks wisdom (understanding), ask God, who gives generously to all ... and it will be given.
(James chapter 1 verse 5)

We have received not the spirit of this world, but the Spirit who is from God, that we might understand the things freely given to us by God. And we impart this in words not taught by human wisdom but taught by the Spirit, interpreting spiritual truths to those who are spiritual.
(1 Corinthians chapter 2 verses 12–13)

Hinduism
Brahman is Reality, Knowledge, and Infinity.
(Taittiriya Upanisad 2.1.3)

One must desire to understand the Infinite (Brahman/God).
(Chandogya Upanisad 7.23.1)

They who know God have left the body behind (abandoned carnal and worldly appetites and sense-desires).
(Svetasvatara Upanisad)

By knowing God there is a falling away of all fetters (attains enlightenment) ... there is cessation of birth and death. By meditating upon Him ... desire is satisfied.
(Svetasvatara Upanisad)

He who knows the Supreme Brahman verily becomes Brahman.
(Mundaka Upanisad 3.2.9)

Islam

(Humanity) does not comprehend any of God's knowledge except what He pleases.
(The Cow chapter 2 verse 255)

The Spirit is one of the things, the knowledge of which is only with God. Humanity has been given only a little knowledge thereof.
(The Journey by Night chapter 17 verse 85)

These parables God has put forward for humanity, but none will understand them except those who have knowledge (of God).
(The Spider chapter 29 verse 43)

God has taught humanity that which it knew not.
(The Clot chapter 96 verse 5)

Jainism

One and eternal is my soul (consciousness), characterized by intuition, insight and knowledge.

(The Lay Person's Inner Voyage: Nityanaimittika-pathavali)

Judaism

Incline your ear unto wisdom, and apply your heart to understanding; yes, if you (thirst) after knowledge, and raise your voice for understanding.... Then shall you ... find the knowledge of God.

(Proverbs chapter 2 verses 2–3,5)

Trust in the Lord with all your heart and mind and do not rely on your own understanding.

(Proverbs chapter 3 verse 5)

Knowledge of the holy is understanding.

(Proverbs chapter 9 verse 10)

The wise accumulate knowledge of the holy.

(Proverbs chapter 9 verse 14)

One who has knowledge uses words sparingly, and one of understanding is of an excellent spirit.

(Proverbs chapter 17 verse 27)

Counsel in the heart ... is like deep water; but one of understanding will draw it out.

(Proverbs chapter 20 verse 5)

Those who seek the Lord understand all things.

(Proverbs chapter 28 verse 5)

A good understanding have all they who keep God's Commandments.
(Psalms chapter 111 verse 10)

Sikhism

By hearing the (Divine) Name truth, contentment and Divine knowledge are obtained.... By hearing the Name, the unfathomable becomes fathomable.... By obeying (God) wisdom and understanding enter the mind. By obeying Him one knows all worlds (seen and unseen).
(The Repetition of the Divine Name: The Japji)

Make ... Divine knowledge thy spiritual guide.
(From the Akal Ustat: Praise of the Immortal)

I have obtained understanding by pondering (reflecting and meditating) on Thy (God's) Word.
(Hymn by Guru Angad)

They who understand God's order (Law) ... are never guilty of egoism.
(Guru Nanak's Japji)

Taoism

Those who have reached the stage of thought (enlightenment, awakening or understanding) are silent. They who have attained to perfect knowledge are also silent.
(Blankness of Mind: Lieh Tzu)

Those who understand themselves (know who they truly are) are enlightened (awake).
(Lao Tzu, Tao Te Ching (The Virtue (*Teh*) of Discrimination) chapter 33)

NDE Accounts

- Humanity is only just beginning to understand Creation.
- Towards the Universe have a childlike wonder and curiosity and a desire to learn and understand its mysteries.
- Hunger and thirst for knowledge, particularly of the spiritual.
- There are some things we as humans do not and cannot understand for a higher purpose. We cannot and do not understand everything in the earthly realm because we are not supposed to.
- The knowledge of the Universe is deceptively simple and apparent and yet in the earthly realm we have difficulty remembering it or perceiving it. This knowledge is filtered out before we are born to enable us to learn and grow from our earthly experiences.
- Open your mind to the Universe and understanding will follow.
- The Universe will guide you and give you understanding, but the soul must remain alert, open and receptive.
- Outside of your physical body, the soul has an instant connection with Divine knowledge and all of its questions will receive instantaneous answers.
- Knowledge of anything I wanted to know was instantly transferred without language.
- I was completely in awe of the beauty of the pure love I was being surrounded by. One of my greatest memories is that of all knowledge being available. If I had a question in my thought, I immediately had the answer.
- In the higher realms, there is no such thing as a question without an accompanying answer. All answers are provided instantaneously, clearly and completely.

- During my experience, I was downloaded with information about every question I had ever had. I received instantaneous knowledge of everything there is to know.
- In the spirit world, the soul is infused with knowledge and understanding.
- I knew and understood how everything worked, the laws, if you will, of that higher dimension.
- I automatically knew things and accepted them without fear or hesitation. It was normal for this new dimension I was now in.
- My soul was plugged into expanded knowledge and awareness, making sense of all of the mysteries of the Universe.
- I emerged from my near death experience with a total understanding of the machinations of the universe and the phrase "Love is the answer; communication is the key."
- I became acutely aware of the immeasurable vastness of the Universe and I knew what Eternity was.
- My spirit observed the entire history and evolution of the Universe as if in a fast-forward film.
- I was given knowledge of many things on different levels, appearing instantaneously in my mind. It's as if the knowledge of the ages all appeared in my mind at once.
- Infused knowledge from the higher realms is simple and logical; it is humans which are prone to over-complication.
- Divine knowledge and eternal Truths are simple to understand; the complexity and difficulty are in the living of them during our earthly experience.
- The white energy of God creates within our soul a knowledge which makes all things clear.

- The Light of God infuses the soul with the depth and breadth of eternal knowledge and the wisdom of the ages.
- You will eventually understand everything and all Truth.
- Death of our body is the extinguishment of our earthly identity and ego, replaced by omniscience and total understanding.
- Upon leaving the body, the soul acquires knowledge of everything. A question is instantaneously answered. You become part of the infinite pure white light.
- The soul understands everything in the higher realms.
- In the spiritual realm, the soul is one with its surroundings and with every other being, sharing all the information and knowledge there is to know.
- The collective consciousness comprises the experiences of all who ever lived, the collective knowledge of all. These collective experiences are omniscient knowledge. Everything that has been thought, spoken and done has been recorded. (Author's Note: This would possibly be akin to the so-called Akashic Records.)
- All religions have been created by Humanity to try to understand what truly cannot be fully understood during this earthly experience.
- I was given knowledge that the Universe is unfolding as it should.
- Upon reaching the opening at the end of the dark tunnel, I experienced the Light, a huge white glow which was massive in size. It was pure, non-judgmental, loving and accepting. Tremendous knowledge was given to me, yet it was not the sort of knowledge you acquire from reading books. It was more like Enlightenment or a meeting with God.

Chapter 19

Loving Nature and All Life-Forms

According to religious scripture cited below, God created the Earth, both animate and inanimate, as well as its interconnected processes. All living things – humanity, animals, plants and trees – are part of God's creation. It is important to love and study Nature as it has much to teach us about ourselves and about God. Knowledge thereof may be found in understanding plant and animal life cycles and the Earth's interconnected ecosystems. As it has been said, if we open ourselves to Nature, Nature will open itself to us. And humanity has been tasked by God to take care of His creation as steward of the natural environment.

Those faiths which accept that God is omnipresent (present everywhere and in all things) and the transcendent reality of which the physical world is but a manifestation, must accept as a corollary the identification of God with, and in, Nature (or Mother Earth) as creator, guardian and benevolent provider. God may be observed not only in human beings but in all sentient beings and in Nature itself. Hinduism and Sikhism stress the need to perceive the Divine in the created world including Nature. Certain Eastern faiths such as Shintoism and various indigenous belief systems believe that everything – all life and natural phenomena and the forces thereof – is imbued with spirit and consciousness, containing aspects of both animism and of pantheism. Zen Buddhism is permeated by a strong connection with Nature, with some panenhenic "all in one" experiences describing a sense of the unity of oneself and Nature. According to Taoism, the actions and processes of Nature are manifestations of the Tao which must be emulated in human life. Reverence for God must therefore include love and respect for the created flora and fauna as well as thanksgiving for the Earth's abundant provision.

The scriptures require humanity to undertake elements of stewardship or guardianship, whereby one should act in a manner that is harmonious with Nature rather than act exclusively for the benefit of oneself, such that one should not take therefrom more than one's basic needs require (a cornerstone of Native American Indian belief and practice). The natural environment provides life itself, sustenance and nurture; connection and context; foundation and orientation. One should therefore work with Nature, not against it, and only utilize its precious resources on a sustainable basis.

That God is in Nature and God is Nature is also affirmed by some of those who have written about their near death experience. They observe the interdependence and connectedness of all spiritual and physical life and existence. Elevated or expanded consciousness perceives God/The Creator/Source not only in other human beings but in all living sentient beings as well as Nature itself. All life and Nature's phenomena are imbued with spirit and consciousness. And, further, that Earth is our mother, a living organism from which humanity can learn much. That we should live in harmony with Nature and only take therefrom what can be sustainably produced is a Universal Law and that humanity's dominion over the Earth's flora and fauna is properly understood as a sacred trust or stewardship. Further, that all life is precious and sacred and should be respected as such and that consciousness extends to trees, plants and animals (which has already been known by indigenous cultures for thousands of years).

At this point in history, humanity must reawaken to its sacred duty as steward/guardian and address the urgent need to re-establish the pristine balance and harmony between

humanity and Nature (before the dire consequences foretold by
the Prophet Isaiah cited below materialize).

Scriptural References
Buddhism

Earth brings us to life and nourishes us. Earth takes us back
again. Birth and death are present in every breath.
(Thich Nhat Hanh's Gathas)

Obey the nature of things and you will walk freely and
undisturbed.
(Sengcan)

Christianity

Behold the birds of the air; they do not sow or reap or store
away in barns, and yet your heavenly Father feeds them.
(Matthew chapter 6 verse 26)

Through Him (God) all things were made; without Him nothing
was made that has been made.
(John chapter 1 verse 3)

For by Him (God) all things were created: things in Heaven and
on earth, visible and invisible ... all things were created by Him
and for Him. He is before all things, and in Him all things hold
together.
(Colossians chapter 1 verses 16–17)

Hinduism

The God who is in fire, who is in water, who has entered the
whole world, who is in plants, who is in trees – to that God be
adoration!
(Svetasvatara Upanisad chapter 2 verses 8–17)

I am omnipresent.... All beings exist in me.... All creatures enter into my nature.... I appear as an onlooker, detached.... Nature gives birth to all moving and unmoving things. I supervise. That is how the world keeps turning.

(Everything is a Sacrifice to Me: Bhagavad-Gita chapter 9)

Islam

Verily, it is God who causes the seed grain and the fruit stone to split and sprout. He brings forth the living from the dead.

(The Cattle chapter 6 verse 95)

To God belongs the kingdom of the heavens and the earth. He gives life and He causes death.

(The Repentance chapter 9 verse 116)

No creature that walks upon the earth is there but its provision is from God. And He knows its dwelling-place.

((Prophet) Hud chapter 11 verse 6)

It is God who sends down water from the sky, which provides you with your drink and brings forth the pasturage on which your cattle feed. And with it He brings forth corn and olives, dates and grapes and fruits of every kind. Surely in this there is a sign for those who think.... It is He who has subdued the ocean, so that you may eat of its fresh flesh.... All this, that you may seek His bounty and render thanks.

(The Bee chapter 16 verses 10–16)

God has made from water every living thing.

(The Prophets chapter 21 verse 30)

God has spread the earth out and set thereon mountains standing firm and has produced therein every kind of lovely

growth (plants).... And God sends down blessed water from the heaven, then God produces therewith gardens and grain (and every kind of harvest) that are reaped.... God gives life therewith to a dead land.
(Qaf chapter 50 verses 7, 9 and 11)

God has made the earth manageable for you, so ... eat of His provision.
(The Kingdom chapter 67 verse 15)

Judaism

God said unto (humanity), replenish the earth, and subdue it: and have dominion over the fish of the sea, and over the fowl of the air, and over every living thing that moveth upon the earth. And God said, Behold, I have given you every herb bearing seed, which is upon the face of all the earth, and every tree, in which is the fruit of a tree yielding seed (for your sustenance). And to every beast of the earth, and to every fowl of the air, and to every living thing that creepeth upon the earth, wherein there is the breath of life, I have given every green herb for (sustenance).
(Genesis chapter 1verses 28–30)

The land is mine and you are but strangers and sojourners. Throughout the country that you hold as a possession, you must provide for the redemption (conservation and management) of the land.
(Leviticus chapter 25 verses 23–4)

You alone are the Lord. You made the heavens ... the earth and all that is on it, the seas and all that is in them. You give life to everything.
(Nehemiah chapter 9 verse 6)

But ask the animals, and they will teach you, or the birds of the air, and they will tell you, or speak to the earth, and it will teach you, or let the fish of the sea inform you. Which of all these does not know that the hand of the Lord has done this? In His hand is the soul of every creature and the breath of all (humanity).
(Job chapter 12 verses 7–10)

Stop and consider God's wonders. Do you know how God controls the clouds and makes His lightning flash? Do you know how the clouds hang poised, those wonders of Him who is perfect in knowledge?
(Job chapter 37 verses 14–16)

The earth dries up and withers, the world languishes and withers, the exalted of the earth languish. The earth is defiled by its people; they have ... broken the everlasting covenant. Therefore a curse consumes the earth; its people must bear their guilt. Therefore earth's inhabitants are burned up, and very few are left.
(Isaiah chapter 24 verses 4–6)

The wild animals honor me, because I provide water in the wilderness and streams in the desert.
(Isaiah chapter 43 verses 20–1)

In wisdom have You (God) made them all; the earth is full of your creatures.... These all look to You to give them food in due season ... when You open Your hand, they are filled with good things (God as the benevolent provider).
(Psalms chapter 104 verses 24, 27–8)

Judaeo-Christian Apocalyptic Literature

Observe ye everything that takes place in the heaven, how they do not change their orbits, and the luminaries (stars) which

are in the heaven, how they all rise and set in order each in its season, and transgress not against their appointed order.
(The Book of Enoch chapter 2 verse 1)

For the waters (rain) are for those who dwell on the earth; for they are nourishment for the earth from the Most High who is in Heaven.
(The Book of Enoch chapter 60 verse 22)

Shintoism
Love nature. Let not humanity subjugate Nature; rather, let humanity be its prudent steward.
(A Coalescent Harmony between Humankind and Nature: Kokutai no Hongi)

Sikhism
Thou (God) art in the tree, Thou art in its leaves. Thou art in the earth.
(Sikh doctrine on the pantheistic conception of God from the Akal Ustat: Praise of the Immortal)

He (God) who created things of different colors, descriptions and species, beholdeth His handiwork which attests to His greatness.
(Guru Nanak's Japji)

Trees, the banks of sacred streams, clouds, fields, islands, peoples ... continents ... lakes, mountains, animals – O Nanak, God knoweth their condition. Nanak, God having created animals taketh care of them all.
(Guru Nanak)

Taoism

Follow the nature of things (including Nature's processes and phenomena).

(The Domain of Nothingness: Chuang Tzu)

(Humanity) is derived from nature, nature is derived from Heaven. Heaven is derived from Tao. Tao is self-derived (self-subsistent).

(Lao Tzu, Tao Te Ching (Describing the Mysterious) chapter 25)

The Ten (Native American) Indian Commandments

Treat the (Mother) Earth and all (living sentient beings) that dwell thereon with respect.

(Commandment No. 1)

Zen Buddhism

Find beauty in imperfection, accept the natural cycle of growth and decay (and regrowth).

(Zen Proverb)

Last year in a lovely temple in Hirosawa, this year among the rocks of Nikko, all's the same to me.

(Satori poem by Hakugai, 1343–1414, Rinzai)

Zoroastrianism

I (Ahura-Mazda/God) have made every land dear to its dwellers, even though it had no charms whatever in it.

(The Creation of the World by Ahura-Mazda)

NDE Accounts

- God is in Nature; God is nature. God is everywhere and within us.
- Behold God in nature.

- Love Nature, study it closely, learn from it and become one with it.
- Love Nature and sanctify all life.
- Behold and rejoice in the beauty of all life forms, as they are all created by God. Like us, they have fear and struggle to survive. So have compassion towards them.
- Tune into Nature and the nature of things.
- Live in harmony with, and deep respect of, Nature.
- Every living sentient creature is one. They must not be harmed. Humanity's dominion over them is to care for, and not exploit or abuse, them.
- Respect all life, including your own. Do not do any harm or injury.
- Your life on Earth is precious. All life is precious.
- You are not less than or greater than any other living sentient being in the world.
- Trees, plants and animals also have consciousness.
- The trees seemed almost alive in a way. It was like they were conscious and communicating with me, like they were happy that I could see them in their true form.
- As a result of my near death experience, I could feel some radiant energy flowing all around me, especially from the trees.... I could feel that I was connected to a mysterious source of energy which was all around me.
- I felt one with Nature – the woods, the fields and our neighbor's livestock. I felt "one" with them all. I "heard" them talk to me and I "talked" right back: a telepathy. Even the trees and blades of grass spoke to me. "See how beautiful and perfect we are. All we have to do is grow and exist and BE. We are all 'one.'"
- All created Beings – flora and fauna – know they were created by the Source.
- Animals have souls. Have respect and appreciation for them.

- Animals have souls and reincarnate.
- Our pets offer us companionship and the opportunity to develop love and compassion for all living beings.
- God's creatures are put on Earth to teach us love, compassion and respect. If we cannot love and respect God's creatures, then how can we love one another and God?
- The Earth is our mother, a living organism.
- Spiritual beings of higher vibration than humans live on Earth as caretakers of its physical life and of the balance of Nature.
- The planet we call Earth has a proper universal name called Gaia which has its own energy and abundance. Humans manipulate Gaia's energy through their choices. The universal laws require us to live in harmony with Gaia's energy and not to take from Nature more than our needs require and what Gaia can sustainably produce.
- Exchange and share love, compassion, energy and light with Gaia which is also a living entity.
- As a result of my near death experience, I was more influenced by pantheism.

Chapter 20

Self-Reflection, Acknowledgment and Awakening (Enlightenment/Self-Realization)

Reflection upon, and acknowledgment of, one's errors and past mistakes and wrongdoing provide opportunities for spiritual growth. As the Zen proverb observes, failing is not always failure as our mistakes provide us with opportunities for growth. This insight is reflected in some of the scriptural references which follow as well as in some of the written accounts of those who have undergone a near death experience. But the common ground stops there. As we shall see, while numerous of the world's faiths and belief systems hold to the view that judgment and forgiveness of the soul belong exclusively to the Divine prerogative, many of the NDE accounts stress that God is Unconditional Love and is therefore not about judgment and punishment. That God would judge or punish is a mere human construct. Rather, in the context of the so-called life-review which each soul undertakes post-physical death, only we can judge ourselves, as we are our harshest critic, with the assistance and guidance of God and the Beings of Light. This process is educational rather than punitive in nature.

From a religious perspective, repentance of wrongdoing involves a feeling of genuine and heartfelt contrition for past misconduct and its harmful consequences. Through a process of internal self-review of one's life (which does not seek to judge or condemn but rather to awaken), the causes of wrongdoing may be identified, understood and renounced and personal responsibility accepted for one's actions and omissions. This is a key tenet indeed of Jainism.

Some religions such as Islam stress that repentance from the tongue must be accompanied by a repentance from the heart. Repentance without renunciation is of no avail. Genuinely and sincerely confessing and repenting one's transgressions in mind, speech and body and seeking God's forgiveness and guidance on how to avoid future wrong, help to heal and restore the right relationship between the believer and God and constitute a form of spiritual renewal or fresh start going forward.

By contrast, many NDE accounts examined refer to the experiencer undergoing what some term a "life-review" in which the soul is shown a replay of the life they have just lived and invited to reflect essentially on what they learned from their life experiences, whether they practiced unconditional love and how they might have acted better towards others. This is important as what lies ahead for us on our soul's evolutionary journey depends on how we lived, and learned from, our most recent incarnation (see Chapter 10 above in which the universal laws of *karma* and reincarnation are explained).

Describing the nature of the life-review may be divided into the substance of what it entails and the process or means by which it is undertaken. In relation to substance, the purpose of the life-review is basically a stock-take or "exit interview" for the edification and evolution of our soul-consciousness. How could we have done better with our time on Earth in that particular incarnation? The Beings of Light typically ask questions such as the following when the soul is watching a replay of their entire life including their thoughts, words and deeds, both positive and negative, and their interactions and experiences with other living beings:

What have you done with your life?
What did you learn and what Divine knowledge did you acquire?

Did you understand what unconditional love is and did you
   practice it?

How did you love, help and care for others?

Did you create joy?

What have you done that was completely selfless in the sense of
   not being motivated by personal gain?

According to the IANDS authors, we are shown those occasions
when we manifested love to others and those occasions when
we hurt others to such a degree that they doubted their self-
worth or were diminished in their own capacity to manifest
love and be loved. Through insensitivity or carelessness, did we
hurt others and how could we have acted differently to secure
the highest outcome for all concerned? We are invited to reflect
on these matters, to acknowledge our "mistakes" and to learn
therefrom. One's conduct is not so much wrong or mistaken
but rather not helpful to the soul's development and that of the
other souls affected.

Souls learn through the life-review that what we consider
important in the Earthly plane – power, wealth and fame – mean
nothing in the Higher Realms; conversely, what we consider
relatively insignificant in the Earthly realm – such as feeding a
stray cat or extending a small kindness to a stranger – may be
the most profound and meaningful. Souls are also taught that
we should never underestimate how impactful our thoughts,
words and deeds are on others and their unforeseen and
extended consequences. Some IANDS authors use the metaphor
of dropping a pebble into the middle of a still pond or pushing a
domino which then cascades forward taking down many other
dominos in quick succession. The choices we make through the
exercise of our Free Will (see Chapter 15) and our thoughts,
words and deeds are indeed powerful and influential, and have
lasting effects on countless others as they ripple outwards or
cascade forward.

But a most important point concerning the life-review is that it is educational rather than condemnatory in nature. It is a journey of self-realization. The only "judgment" which is made on how we lived our life is made by us. We are invited to reflect on our acts and our omissions – things not said or done (which should have been said or done) – in a clear and undistorted light. How could the best and highest outcome for us and those around us have been achieved? There is, of course, nothing to stop us from engaging in a "pre-emptive" or anticipatory life-review right now to enable us to better prepare for what may well lie ahead for us on our soul's evolutionary journey.

As for the actual process involved in a life-review, it typically involves what has been described as a holographic 3-D movie; a panoramic virtually instantaneous review of life's most significant moments. It involves a fast-moving display of visual images and associated feelings and emotions clearly and vividly presented. In one case, the life-review was described as one's life flashing before them like flipping pages of a book. As another IANDS author observes, each soul has a record of every thought, word spoken and act done which forms the basis of the life-review (reminiscent of the so-called Akashic Records and verse 7 of Chapter 98 of *The Book of Enoch*: "Every sin is every day recorded in heaven in the presence of the Most High."). But the soul is much more than a passive observer during the process. The soul witnesses their life from a variety of different perspectives: from a third-party objective observer's point of view, from the soul's point of view and from the perspective of those who were affected by the soul's acts and omissions in positive and negative ways. The soul experiences the thoughts, feelings and emotions of those who were affected by the soul's positive and negative conduct, thereby transcending the soul's own selfish perspective while acquiring the perspective of those who were affected by the soul's conduct and choices. The soul feels respectively the happiness, joy, pain, anger, hurt and sadness of those whom the soul was kind and insensitive to. It is the ultimate exercise in empathy – being in the shoes, so to speak, of others and feeling both the intended and unintended effects of the soul's acts and omissions during its Earthly lifetime.

Scriptural References
Baha'i

All men shall, after their physical death, estimate the worth of their deeds, and realize all that their hands have wrought.
(Baha'u'llah)

You must pray and repent for all that you have done which is wrong; and you must implore and ask for help and assistance; so that you may continue to make (spiritual) progress.
(True Belief: Words of Wisdom from the Supreme Pen of Baha'u'llah)

Buddhism

Evil-doers mourn in this world and they mourn in the next; they mourn in both. They mourn and suffer when they see the evil result of their own work.
(The Dhammapada chapter 1 (The Twin-Verses) verse 15)

If a monk remembers having committed a sin and desires again to be pure, let them reveal the sin committed and when it has been revealed, it shall be well for them.
(Vinaya, Mahavagga, Second Khandaka, chapter II.3.3)

Christianity

There is joy in the presence of the angels of God over one sinner who repents.
(Luke chapter 15 verse 10)

If we confess our sins, God is faithful and just to forgive us our sins and to cleanse us from all unrighteousness.
(1 John chapter 1 verses 9–10)

And the dead were judged by what was written in the books, by what they had done.
(Revelation chapter 20 verse 12)

Islam

Truly, God loves those who turn to Him in repentance.
(The Cow chapter 2 verse 222)

On the Day when every soul finds all the good it has done present before it, it will wish all the bad it has done to be far, far away.
(The Family of Imran chapter 3 verse 30)

Of no effect is the repentance of those who continue to do evil deeds.
(The Women chapter 4 verse 18)

God accepts the repentance of His servants and pardons their sins. He has knowledge of all your actions.
(The Counsel chapter 42 verse 25)

Jainism

As life is so fleet and existence so precarious, wipe off (acknowledge and renounce or confess) the sins you ever committed.
(The Simile of the Leaf: Uttaradhyayana)

For the sake of the splendor, honor and glory of this life, for the sake of birth, death and final liberation, for the removal of

pain, all causes of sin are to be comprehended and renounced in this world. They who, in this world, comprehend and renounce these causes of sin are called a sage.
(Acaranga Sutra: First Book Lecture 1: Knowledge of the Weapon)

Judaism

I will declare my iniquity; I will be sorry (remorseful) for my sin.
(Psalms chapter 38 verse 18)

Those who (cover up) their sins shall not prosper but whoso confesses and forsakes them shall have mercy (forgiveness).
(Proverbs chapter 28 verse 13)

Judaeo-Christian Apocalyptic Literature

I (Enoch) saw the (Lord of Spirits) when He seated himself upon the throne of His glory, and the books of the living were opened before Him.
(The Book of Enoch chapter 47 verse 3)

I (Enoch) observed the heavenly tablets, and read everything which was written (thereon) and understood everything, and read the book of all the deeds of (humanity) ... and after that I said: "Blessed are they who die in righteousness and goodness, concerning whom there is no book of unrighteousness written."
(The Book of Enoch chapter 81 verses 2 and 4)

All the words of your unrighteousness shall be read out before the Great Holy One; and your faces shall be covered with shame.
(The Book of Enoch chapter 97 verse 6)

All your evil deeds are revealed in the heavens, and none of your deeds are covered and hidden.
(The Book of Enoch chapter 98 verse 6)

From the angels He (the Most High) will inquire as to your deeds.
(The Book of Enoch chapter 100 verse 10)

Although you sinners say: "All our sins shall not be searched out and written down," nevertheless they (the heavenly angels) shall write down all your sins every day.
(The Book of Enoch chapter 104 verse 7)

Sikhism
Pardon our errors and mistakes.
(Sri Wahguru Ji Ki Fatah!)

Taoism
The Tao is the good person's (spiritual) treasure, the bad person's last resort.... The reason the Ancients esteemed Tao was because if sought it was obtained and because by it those who have sin could be saved.
(Lao Tzu, Tao Te Ching (The Practice of Tao) chapter 62)

Zoroastrianism
The Law of Ahura-Mazda (God), O Zarathustra (Zoroaster)! takes away from those who confess it the bonds of their sin.
(Forgiveness of Sin)

All that I ought to have thought and have not thought, all that I ought to have said and have not said, all that I ought to have done and have not done … all that I ought not to have thought and yet have thought, all that I ought not to have spoken and yet have spoken, all that I ought not to have done and yet have done … for thoughts, words and works (deeds), bodily and spiritual, earthly and heavenly, pray I for forgiveness and repent of it. (Prayer for Repentance)

NDE Accounts

- Acknowledge your mistakes to learn and grow.
- My life review imparted to me that through our mistakes, we learn.
- You are the victim and beneficiary of all your actions.
- I could see every part of my life, every event all at once. Although it seemed instantaneous, I knew that every moment was there. My hard drive was downloaded, as it were, and my life was replayed in fast forward.
- I learned from my life review that it is not about judgment but rather self-realization and a step in the evolution of the soul in relation to understanding unconditional love and acquiring Divine knowledge.
- There is no judgment during the life review; only reflection.
- Everything I had ever said or done was shown to me. It was like watching a movie reel. God does not judge or condemn us; we judge ourselves.
- There is no condemnation or judgment; only reflection upon how one could have acted differently to secure a better outcome for all concerned.
- The love you give is yours for all eternity; you only answer for your incompletions – all the things not said or done. You observe all the paths not taken in life but which might have been taken.
- During my life review, the Being of Light asked me in a non-verbal manner whether I had loved and how did I treat others.

- Are the things you have created in your life until now worthy of you?
- I was asked: "What have you done with your life? To what extent did you learn to love and assist others? What knowledge did you acquire? Did you do selfish acts or selfless acts?" The process was educational rather than condemnatory in nature. My life review comprised a series of fast-moving pictures akin to slides, clearly and vividly presented.
- The Being of Light asked me what I had done with my life and what I had learned. There was no accusation or condemnation. The soul is invited to reflect on their recent life and encouraged to follow the best pathway.
- A spiritual Being of Light presents the soul with a review of its life to solicit reflection and learning therefrom. It is very rapid, almost instantaneous, similar to a motion picture. A display of visual images and associated feelings and emotions is experienced by the soul.
- I was asked during my life review what I had ever done in my life that was totally selfless? What kind words or deeds were spoken or done that were not motivated by the prospect of personal gain?
- The Being of Light asked me: "What actuated you? Did you act out of righteousness or because it was good for you personally?"
- All of us will eventually be asked three questions: "What did you learn on Earth and how did you help others? Did you create joy on Earth?"
- Our life review also includes things we did not do but which we could and should have done. It is a stock-take for the edification and development of our soul.
- Our life review is like an exit interview, seeing our life as we lived it and understanding things differently in a new light and then moving on.

- Each soul has a record of everything thought, spoken and done. This forms part of the soul's Life Review. Each act of kindness, however small, is recorded.

- Every thing said, thought and done from infancy to death is reviewed before the angels and the Heavenly Light.

- I was shown the review of my entire life: every thought, every word, every action I had thought, said and done during my lifetime on Earth. It was complete in the blink of an eye. All was known and understood. I felt no judgment or condemnation; only unconditional acceptance, peace and love.

- During my life-review, I could see and feel how I had hurt people out of my own carelessness.

- I learned that our actions and words are powerful and possess rippling and lasting consequences.

- I felt and experienced the scenes from my life from the perspectives of all those present.

- One's entire life is witnessed from a third party observer's point of view, from the soul's point of view and that of those who were affected by the soul's acts and deeds. The soul feels the feelings and emotions of those who were affected by the soul's positive and negative conduct. The soul gains the perspective of the humans who were affected by the soul's choices. Even the soul's seemingly innocent choices can have implications beyond which we could ever have imagined. It therefore matters deeply what choices we as humans make in exercise of our gift of free will. One's conduct is not so much wrong but rather not helpful to the soul's development and that of the other souls affected.

- Our life review examines those lifetime events when love most manifested itself and those times when we hurt others to such a degree that they doubted their self-worth or felt diminished in their ability to love and be loved.

- All throughout the life review process, the only entity which judged me was myself. The Light did not praise or condemn my earthly actions or inactions, but paused some scenes and asked for my observations and reflection.
- Each soul is assisted by spirit guides in a review of the soul's immediate past life. There is no judgment, nor is there any punishment. That God would judge or punish is a human construct as God only loves. Only the soul itself is required to judge, evaluate and reflect as it is its harshest critic.
- My angel told me that I must review my life in order to cleanse my soul, and that it is important that I learn from this. The angel told me that my life is evaluated by the most powerful judge there is – that being me!
- One's entire life, including all of the good and bad deeds, are reflected upon in a clear and undistorted light. One's life cannot be misrepresented or lied about. Nothing can be concealed.
- During a panoramic, instantaneous review of the most significant events of the life just lived on Earth, a Being of Light poses a non-verbal question or questions and asks the soul to reflect on and evaluate that life.
- A Being of Light told me that she was God's messenger who was assigned to review my life. She had the ability to reach inside my mind and pull out the memories and events of my life, which we reviewed together like a flickering movie.
- Any guilt or remorse you might feel witnessing your life review is not yours to take or keep.
- A Life Review is re-living and an opportunity to consider what our soul has learned from the incarnation's experiences and interactions. There is no judgment or condemnation. Only we judge ourselves from a perspective

outside ourselves with clear-sighted vision. We discover how profound an impact seemingly insignificant actions had on others and how the exercise of our free will and decision-making ripples outward to countless others. And the hurt we inflict on others in turn causes them to inflict hurt on yet others that we could never have anticipated.

- My life review was a 360-degree movie projection displaying the domino or ripple effects of what harsh and unkind words and deeds have on others and which are passed on to yet others. You feel the anger and sadness of your victims.

- A series of images and experiences were displayed like a projector displaying images on a flat screen. I could see, feel, think, hear and experience the emotions, thoughts and experiences of everyone I had either direct or indirect contact with.

- When I realized that I was dead, my life started flashing through my mind like flipping pages through a book. It seemed to finish in a second. Everything I did and everything I didn't do but could have done was reviewed.

- You don't just observe what you did but you feel the repercussions of your actions – the injury, fears, pain and anger of those who suffered at your hands and the ripple effects they in turn passed on to yet others.

- My life review was like a holographic movie. You are a witness to your own life, an objective observer because you feel the feelings of everyone involved and see each person's point of view rather than your own selfish perspective. Our thoughts, words and deeds are like pebbles dropped in the middle of a pond, sending out ripples to eternity.

- Our actions are like a single drop of water landing in the middle of a pond. It creates ripples which affect not only our immediate interactions but those others with whom they in turn come into contact with. The impacts are often unforeseen and never-ending.

- If you can imagine a series of dominos cascading downwards like water down staggered steps, then this was the experience of being in the shoes of other people and experiencing both the intended and unintended effects of my contact with them. I saw a multitude of opportunities to help people and be loving and kind, but I often chose to ignore those opportunities and instead focus on myself.

- My life review was like watching a movie in which I was the leading actor. You see people who received love from you without you knowing it. You witness the ripple effects of your good deeds. You see all the good deeds done by others because of love shown to them. Small kindnesses result in unforeseen but profound manifestations of love.

- Small acts of kindness count for much in the higher spiritual realms.

- Even small acts of kindness can trigger unforeseen positive consequences for others as the effects thereof ripple outwards.

- What my life review taught me was that the most extraordinary and significant moments of our lives are not what we consider them to be – wealth, possessions, fame, promotions etc. What we consider to be trivial actions or small kindnesses (like feeding a stray cat) are the most significant.

- Placed in front of me to see and feel was my life review … in color. I had to see and feel the good I had done (and the good I didn't even know I did). I could actually feel the joy each person felt when I touched their life in a loving way. Reviewing my random acts of kindness gave me the most joy because I was able to feel the difference I had made in someone's life that I hadn't realized at the time … and I didn't even know them. Little acts of kindness mean so much to God. I also had to see and feel all the hurtful things I had done (even the hurtful things I didn't know I did). I had to feel the person's hurt I had caused. God was not judging me; I was judging myself. I was so ashamed and there was no hiding. God asked me what different choices could and should I have made and what I was learning from my review. This was clearly not the punishing God I had been taught to believe in. Although I was having a hard time forgiving myself, God had already forgiven me. Before we can let God's light and love in, we must forgive ourselves. God wants us to accept His love for us. Once that was revealed to me, I was able to more openly and honestly look at my life. God loves us the way we love our children. Even when they do something wrong, we still love them. Our love for them does not change.

- It was as if I was watching a very complex hologram that showed the story of my life, where I was the hologram, but also watching from a third person perspective. I felt all the pain, loneliness, fear and suffering that had been part of my life, but all of the love too. Everything I had ever done, ever felt, ever had done to me, I relived. I also felt others' feelings as if they were my own. Every time I had hurt someone I felt their pain as my own. Every time I brought happiness to someone, I felt that as if it were my own. I got to see how these people in turn, turned around and either spread the good feeling to someone else, or hurt someone with the pain I had given to them. And then I felt their pain. I was overwhelmed. I was shown many different futures all at the same time. I was also shown years ahead, to the end of my Earthly life and beyond.

Chapter 21

Conclusion

This book has sought to compare (and in a few cases to contrast) the commonly shared messages and observations brought back from the Other Side by those who have undergone a near death experience, with what can be found in the scriptures and afterlife teachings of 12 of the world's great religions. Generally speaking, the similarities and parallels are quite striking and remarkable. The symmetry of the messaging extends across many important themes and concepts including God/The Source, Heaven(s), the Ultimate Reality, interconnectedness, timelessness, positive and negative energies, the immortality and liberation of the soul-consciousness, the Universal Laws of *karma*, reincarnation and attraction, the Golden Rule, Free Will, the inner life, living mindfully in the present moment, our proper relationship with Nature and all living beings, universal knowledge and understanding, and reflecting on and taking responsibility for our wrongdoing. The NDE messaging corroborates in many respects what has long been taught in the sacred scriptures of these religious traditions. This has prodigious implications not only for those who consider themselves to be religious and/or spiritual but also for those who are still searching (or perhaps have abandoned the search). The parallel messaging also provides assurance for the terminally ill, those who fear death, the suicidal and the grieving.

The consistency and uniformity of the messaging across the NDE accounts and religious scripture may be summarized as follows:

- The one and only God/Source/The Light/The Transcendent Supreme Being is the energy of Unconditional Love and

Truth which permeates and connects all things and all of Creation: eternal, changeless, without beginning or end, infinite, incorporeal (an unembodied spirit), all-knowing/ omniscient and the Creator of All That Is. God is the Bestower of all life, imbuing everything with being. God is immanent in the sense of dwelling within our heart and soul and omnipresent in the sense of being everywhere and in all things at the same time.

- Heaven (consisting, it would seem, of various ascending levels) is part of the Ultimate Reality and is described by many IANDS authors as our real or true home. It is dominated by an intensely brilliant golden white Light which appears to have life and identity of its own. Heaven can be considered as a state of mind in which the soul-consciousness experiences pure unconditional love and warmth, understanding, acceptance, peace, contentment, serenity and harmony; as an emotional experience of joy, bliss and euphoria; or a physical description by the soul's sense perception capacities including the vision of beautiful landscapes of clear blue sky and vibrant, unearthly and pulsating colors, smells of fragrant odours and the sounds of mesmerizing unearthly music. It can also be described through a spiritual frame of reference in which negative energy or anything not of the Light (such as fear, pain, suffering, anger, hatred, aggression, wants, needs and desires) is not permitted to enter.

- Belief, faith, hope and trust in God as experienced and practiced in the Earthly realm and as taught in scripture are superseded in the higher spiritual realms by certainty of knowledge of the existence, and awareness, of God. Upon returning from the veil, a near death experiencer no longer needs to have faith in the existence of God because their experience has proven to them the undeniable existence of God, the Earthly sense-perception restrictions having fallen away in the higher spiritual realms. I no longer need to believe because I now know.

- All is an interconnected oneness, although that does not seem real or evident in the Earthly realm where we live in apparent separation and separateness. We perceive our world as comprised of separate objects and living entities. Our Earthly reality is one of dualism in which the observer is separate or removed from what is being observed. But the concept of Universal non-dualism/ oneness/unity is beginning to emerge from recent research in the field of sub-atomic quantum mechanics. According to particle theory, the notion of separation and separateness is complete illusion; every object is connected with every other object through energy and its vibrations. Each particle is connected to every other particle at the deepest foundational level of the Universe. In the spiritual realms, where the "I" or ego does not exist, the observer and the observed cannot be separated as they are an indistinguishable one. As one near death experience account observed, experiencing the Oneness and Unity of God and all of Creation is like awakening from an earthly dream of separation and dualism and feeling a sense of returning Home to the Ultimate Reality. As scripture observes, God is One or a Unity; an immanent or indwelling spirit or energy which connects all things and possesses omnipresent attributes in being everywhere and in all things at the same time. Like an intricate web or mosaic, the soul-consciousness is one with the Universal Consciousness or expansive reality in which all is one and connected.

- Earthly life is but a dream, illusion or appearance; spirit is our reality in which the true nature of things may be more readily recognized. What the eye perceives is temporal; what it cannot see is eternal. Both scripture and the NDE accounts identify God as the Ultimate/One Reality, the One Consciousness. This Ultimate Reality transcends space and time and is self-existent, unchanging and without beginning and end. It is the source of all knowledge – past, present and future – and encompasses everything.

• Linear time and space as they are conceptually understood and experienced on Earth do not exist in the spiritual realms. A moment can seem like an eternity and an eternity a moment. The spiritual realm is non-linear. There is no past, no future, only the present. Yet the present includes the future and the past. Everything that ever happened or is ever going to happen is actually happening at that very moment. Everything is always experienced in the now, including past and future.

• Pervading everything is energy which cannot be created or destroyed and which has always been, and always will be, moving in and through different and ever changing forms. God/Source is universal energy infused into everything, including humans, animals, plants and trees. Everything is created from the same sub-atomic particles connected to Source energy. All living sentient beings are surrounded by their own energy auras. Energy intensity and vibrations vary between spiritual and physical matter (with the latter being lower). Upon the death of our body, our soul-consciousness experiences higher vibrations. We are therefore not merely our Earthly body; we are the energy that is one with that of God/Source. Humanity is continually exposed to both positive and negative energy or what the Abrahamic religions (Judaism, Christianity and Islam) term good and evil or what Hinduism, Jainism and Buddhism refer to as wisdom/enlightenment/

awakening and ignorance. Each soul manifests both positive and negative energy. The types of positive energy identified by the authors of the NDE accounts comprise many of those qualities or attributes which mainstream religions identify as Divine virtues. The most powerful positive energies include unconditional love and kindness, empathy and compassion, charity, goodness, gratitude, joy, acceptance and forgiveness, truthfulness and understanding. Negative energy – such as violence, fear, anger, hatred, aggression, greed, selfishness, guilt, worry, anxiety and being judgmental – is not of God and so does not exist in the higher spiritual realms. Such energy lessens our energy flow, intensity and vibrations and harms our soul. It impedes the Light of God from flowing freely within and through us and ultimately prevents our spiritual elevation and progress.

- The Universal Law of Karma essentially postulates, to borrow from a biblical metaphor, that what we sow is what we ultimately reap. All that we send forth into the Universe is sooner or later returned to us. Karma is the sum of a person's actions in this and previous states of existence which determine their fate in future existences. What happens in a previous life directly impacts the *atma* or soul in the next life, either positively or negatively. According to religious beliefs concerning reincarnation, the soul or spirit, after physical death of the body, begins a new life in a new body that may be human or animal depending on the moral quality of actions from the previous lifetime. However, the unanimous view or conviction of those who have undergone a near death experience is that reincarnation transcends belief and is a certain fact or Universal Law. Reincarnation facilitates the evolution of consciousness – it gives us the opportunity to gradually evolve spiritually through various valuable learning experiences we acquire in our different incarnations. The essence of the Universal Law of Attraction is that like understands and attracts like and that it manifests or creates the things we are thinking of. What we think and speak about and do draws similar energy to us. Positive thoughts, words and deeds attract positive energy unto you; negative thoughts, words and deeds attract negative energy unto you. We become what we think and speak of and do. We create for ourselves what we focus on. In other words, our thoughts, words and deeds create our own reality. What our soul's energy emits draws similar energy back to us, for good or for bad.

• The so-called "Golden Rule" enjoins us to treat others as we would wish to be treated. This concise maxim represents a principle of conduct which has a potentially profound impact on our relations with others and represents a fundamental tenet of many faiths and belief systems. This message was also conveyed to a number of near death experiencers. There are few other ethical exhortations which so forcefully and succinctly capture the essence of how we should interact with other living sentient beings.

• Scriptural references state that each of us has a soul which has been bequeathed to us by God and to whom our soul returns. The soul is eternal and cannot be destroyed. Some of those who have undergone a near death experience report some remarkable observations which corroborate but go far beyond what may be found in religious scripture. They observe consistently that our consciousness survives the death of our physical body and does not depend on a functioning human brain. Our consciousness survives the death of our brain which merely serves as a conduit or filter respectively enabling and limiting access to universal knowledge, awareness and connection to the higher realms. Consciousness is transcendental, limitless and eternal energy; our true essence, our mind, sense-perception, thoughts, feelings and emotions and who and what we truly are at the deepest and most basic level of existence. Consciousness transcends all physical/material matter and is a foundational building-block of all that is and of the Ultimate Reality (see above Chapter 6). Outside of our physical body, our soul is a receptor to elevated awareness and expanded consciousness. Our physical bodies are mere temporary homes enabling us to pursue our Earthly mission.

- Liberation of the soul-consciousness is facilitated by detachment – the antithesis of a desire to acquire and accumulate. It is a detachment from things and objects which are impermanent by nature. Detachment is separation from the ways of this world and all of its distractions and illusions. It is an understanding of the relative unimportance and transient nature of personal power, fame and worldly wealth and pleasures. Detachment is a cessation of desire and craving and a suppression of one's ego. Detachment is a letting go of things which must be parted with in any event on the death of the physical body. We enter this world with nothing and depart therefrom with nothing, apart from the love within the heart and soul accumulated over an incarnated lifetime. Liberation of the soul-consciousness is living a simple and uncomplicated life in the spirit rather than in the world, leading to an expansion of consciousness or spiritual awakening. Numerous accounts of those who have undergone a near death experience point to various fallacious human or Earthly constructs which have been deconstructed for them by their learnings in the higher spiritual realms. We must seek to free ourselves from these illusions in order to recall the true nature of our soul-consciousness and what our Earthly purpose is. This is the path to self-realization and enlightenment.

• According to both scripture and NDE accounts, our physical body is a temple or sanctuary of the Divine spark that dwells in each of us. The human body is a perishable, temporary Earthly vessel or receptacle for our soul-consciousness or life-force which is eternal. Our body enables our soul-consciousness to experience Earthly life and to learn and grow therefrom. What we commonly refer to as death is the separation of the soul-consciousness from the physical body; a shedding of our physical existence and a transition of our soul-consciousness to a spiritually-based experiential existence in which our energy assumes a new form. Our re-birth into the spiritual realms and the Ultimate Reality transitions our soul to heightened and more acute thought, perception, awareness and consciousness, such that things may be perceived as they really are as opposed to how they appear in the Earthly realm. The death of our body is leaving behind our temporary home and returning to our real or true home. It is a natural continuation of an eternal process of our spiritual evolution towards God/Source.

• Free Will is a precious gift bestowed upon each of us by God. The Truth or the right path has been revealed to Humanity; it rests with the individual soul to choose between the light (positive energy) and the darkness (negative energy). Opportunities come our way in life and our particular life experiences are chosen by us. God honors and respects all of the decisions and choices we make for our lives but we remain responsible and accountable for them at the soul level. We are granted Free Will to allow us to succeed and prosper or to blunder our way through life, by letting us make our own choices, informed or influenced by either positive or negative energy, when we reach the proverbial fork in the road. The choices we make either help us to achieve our soul's lifetime mission or take us further away from it. Sometimes we must fall, acknowledge our mistakes and pick ourselves up again for our souls to learn and grow. Free Will is vital to succeeding in our Earthly life's mission and in facilitating our ascendance into the higher spiritual realms. Our Earthly purpose is to grow towards the Divine.

• The mind is very powerful. Our thoughts create our individual reality. Our life is what our thoughts make it. As we think, so we are. If we wish to create a better personal reality for ourselves, we must purify the upstream (our thoughts and thought processes) in order to cleanse the downstream (our words and actions). Possessing and exercising an inner conscience involves the internal and intuitive recognition of the moral or ethical quality of right and wrong (or positive and negative) concerning one's actions, omissions and motives. It is paying heed to that quiet but persistent and uncompromising inner voice, the Divine spark within us, when conducting oneself (or contemplating conducting oneself) contrary to religious desiderata and Divine injunctions or otherwise behaving inappropriately or beyond the bounds of propriety. We must strive to listen and pay heed to the voice of our soul. These inner whisperings must not be suppressed as our Higher Self wants the best for us and our spiritual development. An inner conscience aligns us with the Divine path and moves us forward towards the Light.

And we must also trust our intuition or instincts as that inexplicable but confident knowing may well be based on knowledge gained previously by the soul-consciousness in the spiritual realms. Therefore seek and trust the inner and do not be distracted by the outer; true beauty shines from deep within the soul.

- We awaken to the meaning and joy of our Earthly life through mindfulness and being present in the moment. All things must pass. Since we cannot undo our past and have only tenuous control over the future, our exclusive focus must be an awareness and appreciation of the present moment – the Eternal Now. We must rejoice in its preciousness as it will never come again. Maintaining a focused awareness of what one is doing, thinking and feeling in each moment, unencumbered by reflections of past regrets and anxieties concerning the future, assists us in performing our daily tasks wholeheartedly rather than superficially. As past memories may contaminate our future outlook, it is better to seek refuge in the reality of the present moment. It is in the here and now that we must reconcile ourselves to our past by forgiving ourselves and others; it is in the here and now that we relearn everything from moment to moment and evolve and shape our destiny. Mindfulness penetrates through to the reality underlying worldly appearances and delusions. Through mindfulness and meditation, we free the mind and awaken to the appreciation and joy of our existence. Let every moment be a new beginning. Do not be so concerned with planning the future or worrying about the past that you are forgoing the joys of living fully in the present moment.
- While human knowledge and understanding of the seen physical realm we call Earth have been accumulating for

millennia, we are only now on the threshold of a more profound understanding of Creation and the unseen spiritual realms. Divine understanding is not the same as human understanding; only the former can enlighten or awaken (or remind) the soul-consciousness. Such understanding is knowledge of, and insight into, the Divine. Understanding is perceiving the way things actually are as opposed to the way we perceive them with our limited and limiting Earthly experience and comprehension: observing each phenomenon in its true nature as it actually is, rather than through the prism of material illusion or through the socio-cultural-religious filter of one's lifelong accumulated individual conditioning. Deep or penetrative understanding is the capacity or ability to recognize and comprehend the Truth, the Dharma or the Tao (as the case may be). Many of those who have had a near death experience report that once outside their body, their soul-consciousness instantaneously taps into, or is infused with, the breadth and depth of Divine knowledge, awareness and understanding of the seen and unseen worlds and how they operate and interact with each other. Understanding extends to comprehending and realizing our highest vision of our soul's potential (self-knowledge). Those who understand themselves by knowing who they truly are and where they have come from are enlightened.

• All living things – humanity, animals, plants and trees – are part of God's creation. Those faiths which accept that God is omnipresent (present everywhere and in all things) and the transcendent reality of which the physical world is but a manifestation, must accept as a corollary the identification of God with, and in, Nature as creator, guardian and benevolent provider. Reverence for God and Nature must extend to love and respectful caring for the flora and fauna of this our most beautiful planet as well as gratitude for Earth's abundant blessings. God dwells not only in human beings but in all sentient beings and in Nature itself. The scriptures require humanity to undertake elements of stewardship or guardianship, whereby one should act in a manner that is harmonious with Nature rather than act exclusively for the benefit of oneself, such that one should not take therefrom more than one's basic needs require. That God is in Nature and is Nature is also affirmed by some of those who have written about their near death experience. They observe the interdependence and connectedness of all spiritual and physical life and existence. They also report that elevated or expanded consciousness perceives God/The Creator/Source not only in other human beings but in all living sentient beings as well as Nature itself. Earth is our mother, a living organism from which humanity can learn much. That we should live in harmony with Nature and only take therefrom what can be sustainably produced is a Universal Law. Humanity's dominion over the Earth's flora and fauna is properly understood as a sacred trust or stewardship. Spirit and consciousness also extend to trees, plants and animals (which has already been known by indigenous cultures for thousands of years); therefore all life is precious, beautiful and sacred and should be respected as such.

- Reflection upon, acknowledgment of, and taking personal responsibility for, one's wrongdoing provide opportunities for spiritual growth. Both scripture and the various NDE accounts agree that its root causes must be addressed in order to spiritually progress. Nevertheless, while numerous of the world's faiths hold to the view that an adherent must confess, repent and renounce their wrongdoing and that judgment, punishment and forgiveness of the soul belong exclusively to the Divine prerogative, many NDE accounts stress that God is Unconditional Love and, as such, is not about judgment and punishment. That God would judge or punish is a mere human construct. Rather, in the context of the so-called post-physical death life-review which each soul-consciousness undertakes, only we can judge ourselves (as we are our harshest critic) with the assistance and guidance of God and the Beings of Light. This process is educational rather than punitive in nature. One's conduct is not so much wrong or sinful but rather not helpful to the soul's evolutionary development. The soul is invited to reflect on what it learned from its life experiences and interactions and whether unconditional love and selfless caring for others were understood and practiced. The soul feels empathetically the happiness, joy, pain, anger and hurt of those whom the soul was kind and insensitive to. The soul discovers that what we consider important on Earth means little in the spiritual realms; conversely, what we consider insignificant on Earth is often most profound and meaningful. The soul is also awakened to how impactful our thoughts, words and deeds as well as our omissions are and their potential to inflict unforeseen and enduring consequences. The soul's self-reflection upon these matters is a critical step in progressing its eternal evolutionary journey.

The world's religions have evolved over the millennia from various fundamental underlying principles and tenets including love, compassion, kindness, caring for and serving others, forgiveness, patience, humility, peacefulness, non-violence, restraint of our sense-desires, truthfulness and absence of fault-finding. As such, they provide a moral or ethical compass as well as answers to at least some of the fundamental metaphysical questions alluded to in the introductory chapter. Although the white Light of Truth has been refracted many times in different colors and hues through a prism comprising diverse peoples and their cultures and varying social systems, geographical regions and historical epochs, its source and the essence of its message remain the unchanging same. That this is so has been consistently demonstrated throughout this book by the highly corroborative and reaffirming nature of the observations made by those who crossed over to the Other Side, many of whom reported in their written accounts that prior to their experience, they had no interest in religion or that they were agnostic or avowed atheists. This must surely be reassuring to a confused Humanity today which is being pulled in so many different directions by so many discordant messages and voices.

I (Enoch) know another mystery, that books shall be given to the righteous and the wise to become a cause of joy and uprightness and much wisdom. And to them shall the books be given, and they shall believe in them and rejoice over them, and then shall all the righteous who have learnt therefrom all the paths of uprightness be recompensed.

(The Book of Enoch chapter 104 verses 12–13)

Author Biography

Douglas Hodgson is a dual citizen of Canada and Australia and a retired lawyer and Dean and Professor of Law residing in Perth, Western Australia. He undertook postgraduate legal study at the University of London before embarking on a 35-year career in higher education in Australia, New Zealand and Canada as a teacher, researcher, scholar, author and university administrator. His areas of expertise include Public International Law, International Human Rights Law, International Humanitarian Law, Civil Law and Causation Law. Professor Hodgson has authored and published 30 peer-reviewed law journal articles and six books:

The Human Right to Education
(Dartmouth, Aldershot, Hampshire, England, 1998)
ISBN: 1-85521-909-3

Individual Duty within a Human Rights Discourse
(Ashgate, Aldershot, Hampshire, England, 2003)
ISBN: 0-7546-2361-0

The Law of Intervening Causation
(Ashgate, Aldershot, Hampshire, England, 2008)
ISBN: 978-0-7546-7366-8

International Human Rights and Justice
(Nova Science Publishers, Inc., New York, NY, USA, 2016)
(Editor and Contributor)
ISBN: 978-1-63484-709-4

Transcendental Spirituality, Wisdom and Virtue: The Divine Virtues and Treasures of the Heart
(John Hunt Publishing, Winchester, Hampshire, England, 2023)
ISBN: 978-1-80341-143-9

Spiritual Revelations from Beyond the Veil: What Humanity Can Learn from the Near Death Experience
(John Hunt Publishing, Winchester, Hampshire, England, 2023)
ISBN: 978-1-80341-340-2

Professor Hodgson's professional networks included the Australian Academy of Law, the Council of Australian Law Deans, the Global Law Deans' Forum and the Australian Research Council. He also served as an advisor to the Australian Red Cross, editor of several law journals and as a member of various university human research ethics committees. He was also a regular attender of the Oxford Round Table symposia where he delivered addresses on the concept of an international rule of law, the protection of children's international human rights and the challenges posed by religious fundamentalism to the public school system from a human rights perspective.

As a complement to his work on religious discrimination issues in the educational field, he developed a keen interest in studying and comparing the scriptures of the world's religions and distilling therefrom common and unifying spiritual principles upon which these great and diverse religions are based, ultimately inspiring him to write *Transcendental Spirituality, Wisdom and Virtue: The Divine Virtues and Treasures of the Heart*.

His interest in transcendental spirituality has strengthened and expanded in his retirement years to include the so-called "near death experience" and what humanity can learn from those who have returned from beyond the veil and recounted their experiences and observations. This led to the writing of *Spiritual Revelations from Beyond the Veil: What Humanity Can Learn from the Near Death Experience* in which these observations and insights have been collated, analyzed and commented upon.

In this the final instalment of his spirituality trilogy, Professor Hodgson analyzes and comments upon the remarkable similarity in the messaging shared across, and common between, the written accounts of those who have undergone a near death experience and the sacred scriptures of the world's mainstream religions and faiths.

Sources

IANDS, International Association for Near-Death Studies, Inc. https://iands.org/ndes/nde-stories.html (NDE Accounts)

Internet Sacred Text Archive (ISTA) http://www.sacred-texts.com

N. Smart and R. Hecht (eds) *Sacred Texts of the World: A Universal Anthology* (Quercus Publishing, London, UK, 2007)

F. Masumian "World Religions and Near-Death Experiences" in J. Miner Holden, EdD, B. Greyson, MD, and D. James, RN/ MSN (eds) *The Handbook of Near-Death Experiences: Thirty Years of Investigation* (Praeger Publishers, Santa Barbara, California, USA, 2009)

M. Borg (ed.) *Jesus and Buddha: The Parallel Sayings* (Duncan Baird Publishers, London, UK, 2008)

S. Kapadia *The Teachings of Zoroaster* (John Murray Publishers, London, UK, 1905)

E. Hammond *The Splendour of God (Extracts from the Sacred Writings of the Baha'is)* (E.P. Dutton and Company, New York, NY, USA, 1909)

D. Field *The Religion of the Sikhs* (John Murray Publishers, London, UK, 1914)

D. Goddard and H. Borel *Laotzu's Tao and Wu Wei* (Brentano's, New York, NY, USA, 1919)

F.M. Muller (translator) *The Dhammapada: A Collection of Verses*, Volume 10, Part I, *The Sacred Books of the East* (Clarendon Press, Oxford, UK, 1881)

E.H. Palmer (translator) *The Qur'an*, Volumes 6 and 9, *The Sacred Books of the East* (Clarendon Press, Oxford, UK, 1880)

H. Jacobi (translator) *Jaina Sutras, The Uttaradhyayana Sutra and The Sutrakritanga Sutra*, Volume 45, Part II, *The Sacred Books of the East* (Clarendon Press, Oxford, UK, 1895)

R. H. Charles (translator) *The Book of Enoch* (Dover Publications, Garden City, New York, USA, 2007)

Recommended Reading

Raymond A. Moody Jr., MD *Life After Life* (HarperOne, New York, NY, USA 10007, 2015)

Eben Alexander, MD *Proof of Heaven: A Neurosurgeon's Journey into the Afterlife* (Pan Macmillan Australia Pty Ltd, Sydney, NSW, Australia, 2012)

O-BOOKS

SPIRITUALITY

O is a symbol of the world, of oneness and unity; this eye represents knowledge and insight. We publish titles on general spirituality and living a spiritual life. We aim to inform and help you on your own journey in this life. If you have enjoyed this book, why not tell other readers by posting a review on your preferred book site?

Recent bestsellers from O-Books are:

Heart of Tantric Sex
Diana Richardson
Revealing Eastern secrets of deep love and intimacy to Western couples.
Paperback: 978-1-90381-637-0 ebook: 978-1-84694-637-0

Crystal Prescriptions
The A-Z guide to over 1,200 symptoms and their healing crystals
Judy Hall
The first in the popular series of eight books, this handy little guide is packed as tight as a pill bottle with crystal remedies for ailments.
Paperback: 978-1-90504-740-6 ebook: 978-1-84694-629-5

Shine On
David Ditchfield and J S Jones
What if the aftereffects of a near-death experience were undeniable? What if a person could suddenly produce high-quality paintings of the afterlife, or if they acquired the ability to compose classical symphonies? Meet: David Ditchfield.
Paperback: 978-1-78904-365-5 ebook: 978-1-78904-366-2

The Way of Reiki
The Inner Teachings of Mikao Usui
Frans Stiene
The roadmap for deepening your understanding of the system of Reiki and rediscovering your True Self.
Paperback: 978-1-78535-665-0 ebook: 978-1-78535-744-2

You Are Not Your Thoughts
Frances Trussell
The journey to a mindful way of being, for those who want to truly know the power of mindfulness.
Paperback: 978-1-78535-816-6 ebook: 978-1-78535-817-3

The Mysteries of the Twelfth Astrological House
Fallen Angels
Carmen Turner-Schott, MSW, LISW
Everyone wants to know more about the most misunderstood house in astrology — the twelfth astrological house.
Paperback: 978-1-78099-343-0 ebook: 978-1-78099-344-7

WhatsApps from Heaven
Louise Hamlin
An account of a bereavement and the extraordinary
signs — including WhatsApps — that a retired
law lecturer received from her deceased husband.
Paperback: 978-1-78904-947-3 ebook: 978-1-78904-948-0

The Holistic Guide to Your Health
& Wellbeing Today
Oliver Rolfe
A holistic guide to improving your complete health,
both inside and out.
Paperback: 978-1-78535-392-5 ebook: 978-1-78535-393-2

Cool Sex
Diana Richardson and Wendy Doeleman
For deeply satisfying sex, the real secret is to reduce the heat,
to cool down. Discover the empowerment and fulfilment
of sex with loving mindfulness.
Paperback: 978-1-78904-351-8 ebook: 978-1-78904-352-5

Creating Real Happiness A to Z
Stephani Grace
Creating Real Happiness A to Z will help you understand
the truth that you are not your ego
(conditioned self).
Paperback: 978-1-78904-951-0 ebook: 978-1-78904-952-7

A Colourful Dose of Optimism
Jules Standish
It's time for us to look on the bright side, by boosting
our mood and lifting our spirit, both in our interiors,
as well as in our closet.
Paperback: 978-1-78904-927-5 ebook: 978-1-78904-928-2

Readers of ebooks can buy or view any of these bestsellers by
clicking on the live link in the title. Most titles are published
in paperback and as an ebook. Paperbacks are available in
traditional bookshops. Both print and ebook formats are
available online.

Find more titles and sign up to our readers' newsletter at
www.o-books.com

Follow O books on Facebook at **O-books**

For video content, author interviews and more, please subscribe to our YouTube channel:

O-BOOKS Presents

Follow us on social media for book news, promotions and more:

Facebook: O-Books

Instagram: @o_books_mbs

X: @obooks

Tik Tok: @ObooksMBS

www.o-books.com